READING THE ECONOMIC TEA LEAVES

Secrets to Unlocking the Value of Economic Indicators

JASON SCHENKER

Steve, enjoy the book!

— Jason Schenker

READING THE ECONOMIC TEA LEAVES

Secrets to Unlocking the Value of Economic Indicators

BY JASON SCHENKER

ISBN: 978-1-946197-42-9 *Paperback*
      978-1-946197-49-8 *Ebook*

For budding economists everywhere.

CONTENTS

CONTENTS

CONTENTS

CONTENTS

CONTENTS

READING THE ECONOMIC TEA LEAVES

This is a book about economic reports.

And helping you understand their value.

This book is primarily based on my experiences with economic data while working in investment banking as a trading desk economist as well as my experience running the top-ranked economic and financial forecasting firm Prestige Economics.

I have been analyzing, forecasting, and discussing economic indicator reports and economic data for over 15 years. And during that time period, I have been creating, analyzing, and forecasting financial markets, the economy, company data, and industry data. This includes work I have done for Fortune 500 companies, large industry groups, governmental entities, central banks, and NGOs.

Plus, I have also been at the helm of Prestige Economics, which has been responsible for creating economic indicators and economic reports.

It is a pleasure for me to share my knowledge and experience of economic indicators and economic data with you.

The main goal of *Reading the Economic Tea Leaves* is to introduce you to the value of, the sources of, and the nuances of the most important economic reports and data.

In order to do this effectively, I openly share my greatest learnings and the best practices that have worked for me. I also share challenges I have experienced and the pitfalls you need to avoid when working with economic reports and economic data.

This book has been carefully crafted to provide digestible explanations of complex concepts. To meet these goals, I have structured a mix of explanations, anecdotes, pictures, and graphics to provide context and relevance to what can be an otherwise daunting set of data topics.

Acknowledgements

I want to acknowledge and thank all of the people who were involved in one way or another with the process of making this book come together. First, I want to thank **Nawfal Patel** and my other colleagues at Prestige Economics who helped me bring this book to fruition.

Also, I want to thank **Kerry Ellis**, our cover designer, for bringing my ideas for the cover of this book to life. It was my intention that the cover would convey the complexity and simplicity of reading the oft-referenced notion of reading the economic tea leaves. I am thrilled that we got there!

Additionally, I need to thank the wonderful and talented people at **LinkedIn Learning**, including Jolie Miller, Megan Russell, Dianne Starke, and many others! This book was created as a companion to a course I recorded in 2018 titled Economic Indicators Weekly. If you like this book, you will really enjoy the online course!

You can find this LinkedIn Learning course online: **https://www.linkedin.com/learning/economic-indicators-weekly/**

Finally, and most importantly, I want to thank my family for supporting me as I worked on this book. I am always most grateful for the support of my loving wife, **Ashley Schenker**, and to my parents, **Janet and Jeffery Schenker**.

My family has supported me in countless ways over the years by providing emotional support and editorial feedback.

Every time I write a book, it's a crazy experience that spills over into my family life, so to them and to everyone else who helped me in this process, thank you!

Finally, thank you for buying this book.

I hope you enjoy *Reading the Economic Tea Leaves*!

~ Jason Schenker

READING THE ECONOMIC TEA LEAVES

The big idea of this book is to share how economic data and reports offer insight into industry activity, business activity, and financial market activity. The purpose of this book is to share how these reports and data can have important ramifications for businesses as well as individuals.

I have often described economic data like the staircases from the Harry Potter book series. These staircases are dynamic. I use this analogy because the economy is also dynamic. And there is a way in which some economic data series impact others — the way some data lead others.

Obviously, not all economic reports are critical.

But many of them have significant value. Some, like jobs, retail sales, and GDP have broader economic implications than sector data. And understanding how each report has value is critical to forming a holistic picture of the economy at any point in time.

With three business news television channels and countless business print media outlets, there is often an incentive to make every single economic report, data series, or speech seem earth shattering and market moving.

In that respect, some data releases are like Tevye's staircases that sometimes lead nowhere just for show — or, in this case, a show.

With all the economic indicators and economic data in the world available, it is important to know which reports matter most — and why. And the more economic data and reports there are, the more difficult it can be to derive value from them.

Knowing the difference between Harry Potter and Tevye staircases is important.

In order to help familiarize you with the most important economic indicators, I have divided *Reading the Economic Tea Leaves* into ten sections:

- **OVERVIEW AND IMPACT OF ECONOMIC INDICATORS**
- **LEADING ECONOMIC DATA**
- **THE IMPORTANCE OF POLICY**
- **EMPLOYMENT AND JOBS DATA**
- **OTHER CRITICAL ECONOMIC DATA**
- **HOUSING DATA**
- **GDP GROWTH DATA**
- **MONETARY POLICY**
- **INFLATION REPORTS**
- **PULLING EVERTHING TOGETHER**

This book is the twelfth book I have written in the past 12 months. And it is twice as long as the others, which is the reason this book has more sections than previous books I have written.

The division of sections and brevity of some chapters is designed to help add the most practical value for a reader who may — or may not — be familiar with economic indicators. In that way, this book should add value for someone with even only the most basic understanding of the economy.

In the first section of *Reading the Economic Tea Leaves*, **Overview and Impact of Economic Indicators**, I discuss the most fundamental aspects of economic indicators, like their purpose, origins, type, and value. I also discuss how economic indicators can have important implications and impacts on jobs, sectors, and investments.

In the second section, **Leading Economic Data**, I discuss the most important economic indicators that lead overall economic activity and financial markets. At the top of this list are global purchasing manager indices. The three most important are in manufacturing, and they are the U.S. ISM Manufacturing Index, the Eurozone Manufacturing PMI, and the Chinese Caixin Manufacturing PMI. There are also two other important economic indicators of a similar nature, the U.S. ISM Non-Manufacturing Index as well as the German Ifo. I also discuss the importance of consumer confidence in the United States as well as the Leading Economic Indicators Index from the Conference Board as other valuable leading economic data.

The third section of this book is dedicated to **The Importance of Policy.** This section includes both specific and broader topics of policy. I discuss two important practical policy inputs for the economic outlook. First are the IMF's quarterly World Economic Outlook, which includes global and country GDP growth forecasts. The second practical policy factor I discuss is OPEC. Then, at a broader, more comprehensive level. I discuss monetary policy and fiscal policy.

The fourth section of *Reading the Economic Tea Leaves* is titled **Employment and Jobs Data.** This section includes a chapter about the most critical monthly U.S. economic report — the Employment Situation report, which is often simply called the "jobs report." There are also chapters dedicated to weekly jobless claims and a discussion of various other employment reports and data.

In the fifth section of this book, **Other Critical Economic Data,** I discuss economic reports beyond leading PMIs and critical jobs data that are important to watch with broad macroeconomic implications. These reports include retail sales, vehicle sales, and industrial production.

The sixth section of *Reading the Economic Tea Leaves* is titled **Housing Data;** I discuss some of the most important housing reports and data. These reports are important because housing is an important contributor to GDP. Plus, most consumers' largest assets and self-perception of wealth and economic security is the value of their homes. The collapse in housing was a critical factor for the deep and protracted nature of the Great Recession.

Unfortunately, in many ways, housing has never fully recovered.

In this book's seventh section, **GDP Growth Data**, I discuss some critical facts about GDP, the four parts of GDP, and the difference between GDP and GNP. One of the biggest issues with GDP data is that its release is often slow and data revisions are frequent.

The eighth section of *Reading the Economic Tea Leaves* is titled **Monetary Policy**. In this section, I discuss central bank policies with a focus on the U.S. Federal Reserve in chapters that examine Fed decisions, forecasts, dotplots, Fedspeak, testimony, and regional data. I also discuss the international dynamics of other central banks and their balance sheet policies.

In this book's ninth section, **Inflation Reports**, I focus on the different kinds of inflation as well as on the most critical reports about inflation in the United States. This includes consumer inflation in the CPI report, the importance of the PCE report for the Fed, producer inflation in the PPI report, U.S. energy reports, and the importance of the yield curve.

In this book's tenth and final section, **Pulling Everything Together**, I tie in themes throughout this book across topics to present some important actionable recommendations with corporate, industry, professional, individual, and global implications. The topics in this section include a discussion of inflation and monetary policy, watching for recessions, long-term risks and opportunities, as well as data challenges and how to create data.

In sum, the ten sections of this book should help you understand the most important dynamics when dealing with economic indicators, reports, and data. And they should help you develop a comprehensive and holistic understanding as to how the puzzle pieces of the economy fit together.

Being fluent in economic dynamics is always a positive professional attribute. And having a solid understanding of the dynamics in *Reading the Economic Tea Leaves* can help you in your professional life. Plus, it is also likely to help you think about important decisions that affect you personally, like housing decisions, career choices, and investment risks and opportunities.

WHY I WROTE THIS BOOK

As an economist, I look at economic indicators and data reports all day, every day. And I spent more than 15 years learning the tricks of the trade.

This book is my attempt to give back and share those tricks with you. It's something I am very passionate about.

In fact, I named my economic research firm Prestige Economics, because the etymological origins of the word Prestige are tied to the word "trick." In other words, I firmly believe that there is a trick to understanding the economy, it's something my own research firm shares with our clients on a regular basis, and it's something I wanted to share with you in this book.

If you don't work with economic data now, chances are you will sometime soon. After all, the government, industry groups, professional organizations, central banks, and other parties we are constantly creating ever-increasing volumes of economic indicators, reports, and data.

And companies, governments, and individuals are increasingly digging into data to identify important relationships, uncover valuable business implications, and inform critical decisions.

I wrote this book to help people who analyze economic data, use economic data, and make important decisions with that data.

In this book, I wanted to share what I know and have experienced in a way that could help prepare others to avoid the mistakes I have made with economic data so that they can be at the top of their game more quickly.

Those are the big value-add reasons I wrote this book. But on a more pragmatic level, one of the main reasons I wrote this book was that a lot of the material was already written as part of the preparation to record a weekly Economic Indicators video series with LinkedIn Learning. It would have been a shame to have not pulled those materials together to help learners who may prefer to read about economic indicators than watch video courses online.

In many ways, this book is a collection of insights that I have shared with numerous clients, industry groups, NGOs, and government entities over the years.

In hindsight, I should have written this book years ago. But I have been busy building out the research offerings and client base of my firm Prestige Economics for more than a decade.

In fact, a number of topics in this book are tied to reports and research that we produce on a regular basis.

Even though I could claim to have been too busy to write this book, everyone seems busy today.

And the main reason this book never got written is because I didn't carve out the time to write it.

But now I have.

And why am I the one to write this book?

My background as an economist and financial market forecaster is probably the most important qualification. In addition to having earned a Master's in Applied Economics, Bloomberg News has ranked me and my firm Prestige Economics as one of the top financial forecasters in the world in 43 categories since 2011. And Bloomberg even ranked me #1 in the world in 25 of those categories — many of them multiple times.

I am very proud to have forecasted many things well. But I have made many errors with data over the years. And if I had this book at my disposal when I became a professional economist in an investment bank back in 2004, I would have been able to accelerate my career.

And now that this book has been written, I hope this book helps accelerate your career!

Overview and Impact
of Economic Indicators

CHAPTER 1

THE PURPOSE OF ECONOMIC INDICATORS

The economy is like oxygen.

It's all around you — even if you don't think about it.

It impacts your professional options, your investments, and whether or not you have a job.

And you need to understand what's going on in the economy in order to make important decisions about your company, your career, and your investments.

This book will help you understand where to find the most valuable economic reports as well as what the most important numbers to watch in each report are.

This is all so you can make the best decisions possible.

In this book, you will learn about dozens of important economic indicators that will help you understand what's going on in the economy — and how each indicator impacts your personal, professional, and financial life.

We'll look at reports that cover big economic concepts — like growth, unemployment, and inflation.

We'll examine important economic sector data, like home sales and auto sales.

And we'll dig into economic data that hits your wallet — like how interest rates can affect what you pay for a mortgage, how stock prices trade, and how strong your currency is.

This book is focused on the practical value of economic data. So don't worry, we won't be doing any weird formulas with Greek letters in this book.

But, we're talking about economic reports that you can easily access online, that have data you will be able to understand and apply.

By the end of this book, you might not be ready for an interview on Bloomberg Television or CNBC to discuss the latest employment report, but you'll be aware of data that you may never have known existed.

And you'll know how to find value in that data.

There's an old joke that economists are too smart for their own good, but not smart enough for anyone else's.

Sometimes that's true.

But it won't be in this book!

In this book, I will turn that joke on its head, so you get smart about economics — for your own good, and so you can help others.

With that in mind, let's get started!

CHAPTER 2

ORIGINS OF ECONOMIC INDICATORS

When Bill Clinton was president, it's rumored he had a sign on his desk that said, "It's the economy, stupid!"

Let's face it, we all need to be smart about the economy.

And the best way to know more about the economy is to be familiar with important economic reports that are released on a regular basis — like reports about new home sales, inflation, and unemployment.

These reports are also called economic indicators.

And the numbers in these reports can impact how your financial investments perform.

Plus, these indicators can reveal if your industry will grow, and they can offer insights into your job prospects, like if you might lose your job just because of "the economy."

Economic indicators are reports that are published on a regular basis — like a magazine.

So where do these economic indicators, data, and reports come from?

Well, they tend to come from one of four different places:

Data from Governments

The most common source of economic data is a government like the United States. The U.S. government releases reports through a number of different government entities, like the Bureau of Labor Statistics and the Bureau of Economic Analysis.

In Europe, a lot of data comes from Eurostat, but some data is also released by national governments — like Germany or France.

Data from Central Banks

The second most common source of data is a central bank. These aren't like the main branch of the bank where you have a savings account. These are the banks that set monetary policy and determine important interest rates for an entire economy.

Some central banks include the European Central Bank, the Bank of England, the Bank of Japan, the Reserve Bank of Australia (RBA), the U.S. Federal Reserve (also known as the Fed), and others.

Data from Industry Groups

The third source of economic data is an industry groups or company. If you work in real estate, you might be familiar with the U.S. existing home sales data that comes from the National Association of Realtors.

And if you are in the supply chain world, you might be interested in the Institute for Supply Management's Purchasing Manager Index (PMI), or the material handling industry's Business Activity Index (MHI BAI) that my company Prestige Economics produces on material handling activity in the United States.

Data from NGOs

Finally, there are NGOs — nongovernmental organizations — which are important nonprofits that provide useful economic data.

This often includes big global macro data.

The International Monetary Fund produces important global growth forecasts, OPEC releases monthly oil reports, and demographic data released by the United Nations.

Where the Data Come From

Most economic reports and data can be found online, and there is a full list of where to find a lot of economic indicators throughout this book and in a Data Appendix.

And a lot of important U.S. data can be found at the U.S. Federal Reserve Economic Database — or FRED.

Here is the website: **https://fred.stlouisfed.org/**

FRED also includes a number of important international data series as well.

It is probably the single most important repository of economic data in the world right now. I personally use it almost every day.

Getting to Know Economic Indicators

Once you get to know the indicators, like GDP, which is short for "gross domestic product" and is an important measure of economic growth, you'll probably have a few others that you want to watch regularly.

Maybe housing is your thing, or oil inventories, or auto sales.

Whatever your jam is, there's data for you!

And the best part is that a lot of this data comes from government organizations that will be happy to talk to you on the phone if you have questions about the reports.

It's often your tax dollars at work, so don't hesitate to call the U.S. Bureau of Labor Statistics, Eurostat, or any of the other sources of government or NGO data.

The same is true for industry data.

Industry groups are also usually very happy to talk to you about their data. If you have questions, just send an email — or even better, just give them a call.

If you can't wait to get started, take a look at the list of websites I've provided in the Data Appendix.

It's a data smorgasbord.

Enjoy the feast!

CHAPTER 3

LEADING, LAGGING, AND COINCIDENT INDICATORS

There are three kinds of economic indicators: leading indicators, lagging indicators, and coincident indicators.

There is often a debate about what data fall into which category.

Leading Indicators
These are the most important economic indicators, because as their name indicates, they lead economic activity — and they often lead financial market dynamics.

Economic indicators like Purchasing Manager Indices (PMIs), weekly jobless claims, and housing starts are several important examples of indicators that lead the overall economy and specific industries, respectively. I discuss these economic reports and other leading indicators throughout this book.

And there are other financial market indicators like the yield curve, which are often seen as critical predictors of economic growth and recession. This is the subject of Chapters 52 and 54.

In general, leading economic indicators are the most important for corporate strategists and financial investors, because leading indicators offer a glimpse into the future.

Coincident Indicators
Some economic indicators offer good insight into the current state of the economy. A good example of coincident economic indicators include industrial production and retail sales.

Some economists might argue that another coincident economic indicator is gross domestic product, or GDP. By definition this makes sense, since GDP is a measure of total activity across an entire economy.

GDP is growth.

It is the business cycle.

But while some may say GDP is a coincident economic indicator — because it reflects current growth — there is also some logic for the counterargument that GDP is almost a lagging indicator, due to a lag in the way GDP data are collected and the delay with which reports are released.

This is part of a broader discussion in Chapter 34.

Lagging Indicators
While some economic indicators lead overall activity and financial markets, other economic indicators lag behind the overall economy and financial markets.

One of the most widely accepted lagging economic indicators is the unemployment rate. After all, the unemployment rate is often low or falling during recessions, and yet it often rises even after recessions and growth resumes. This dynamic can be seen in Figure 3-1.

Aside from the general discussion of leading, coincident, and lagging economic indicators, there is an actual monthly report called the Leading Economic Indicators report from The Conference Board that includes a number of indicators. Some of these are leading, as the name of the indicator indicates. But some are coincident. And some are lagging. This monthly report is the focus of Chapter 15.

Figure 3-1: U.S. Unemployment Rate as a Lagging Indicator[1]

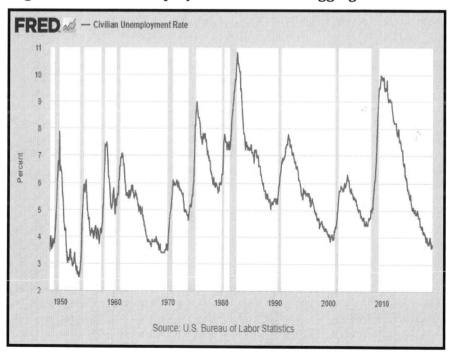

CHAPTER 4

THE VALUE
OF ECONOMIC INDICATORS

When I think of the importance of economic indicators, it reminds me of running with the bulls in Pamplona, Spain. Not the part where everyone is running down a narrow via trying not to get trampled.

It reminds me of what happens after you run down the street with the bulls, because at that point, you are in the arena and bulls are running around and after you.

I was quite a bit younger and a bit more foolish when I did this, but in the arena one guy saw a bull charging at him and he put his hands up in front of his eyes. Of course, this didn't make the bull go away, and the guy got trampled.

This is you if you aren't watching out for the most important economic indicators. If you have ever looked for a job, bought a house, got a loan, or made a business investment, then the state of the economy has impacted you — and you might not have even known it.

In this chapter, let's take a look at why economic reports matter to you personally, to financial markets, and to your company.

I want you to become familiar with and be able to interpret some of the most important data.

First off, let's look at something everyone cares about: housing. Anyone who owns a house or is thinking of buying a house cares about home prices. Plus, home prices are impacted — like all markets — by current supply and demand, as well as expected future supply and demand.

There are a lot of different pieces of housing data here, and they're a bit like a puzzle. And data puzzles matter.

Each of these pieces is spread across a number of monthly economic reports including new home sales, existing home sales, housing starts, building permits, and other reports.

Getting familiar with this data before buying a house — or making a rent versus own decision — could be valuable.

Several years ago, I sold a condo of mine just before the Great Recession. I knew it was coming, and that condo lost 75 percent of its value in the following six months. It saved me a lot of money knowing what was coming down the road.

If you work at a construction company and you are considering buying new equipment or hiring new people, you would probably also want to be looking at housing data on a regular basis.

A close friend of mine was thinking of becoming a real estate developer in late 2007. He asked me about that decision because he knew that I watch data like a hawk. I told him to hold off, and it saved his nest egg from breaking. It saved him hundreds of thousands of dollars.

And there's a similar kind of data puzzle for the job market.

If you were thinking about a career in healthcare, it would be important to know what the forecasts are for growth in the medical field. And you might want to know about the unemployment rates for the states or cities where you would consider working.

And the same would be true if you were an investor looking to buy stock in a retail business like Walmart, Target, or Amazon. You would want to know how the sector is doing and the economic health of the regions it operates in.

As you can see, there are a lot of different data points to consider — and this is true whether you are thinking about your living situation, your profession, your investments, and your future.

Putting your hands up in front of your face doesn't make a raging bull go away. And it doesn't make economic realities vanish either. You need to do what I did in Pamplona in 1997, and grab the bull by the horns. You need to get with the economic indicator program, and start watching national, regional, and industry reports that matter the most to you. The good news is that when you grab the economic indicator bull by the horns, you probably won't be drooled on!

CHAPTER 5

IMPACTS ON JOBS

Are you a recent graduate? Looking for a job? Thinking about changing jobs?

If you are hot on the trail for where your next professional opportunity lies, you need data! Data about the economy, the labor market, and different industries.

Fortunately, there is a lot of great data in monthly government reports about the job market and reports about different economic sectors.

Whether you work in retail, real estate, autos, healthcare, or finance, there are economic reports that offer insight into how your sector is doing — and what opportunities there may be elsewhere in the economy.

In this chapter, we'll talk about the two kinds of data you need to watch to assess the potential and limitations of your career prospects: national or regional job market data and sector data.

National and regional jobs data show how many people are employed and have jobs, as well as the number of unemployed people who want jobs but can't get them. A labor market with low unemployment is tight. There is a low supply of available workers — because basically everyone has a job.

The fewer unemployed people there are in a region, the stronger that job market is — and the more options you will have to either get a job or be paid more for a job you already have. You have more professional leverage.

In a region with high unemployment, however, you are likely to have fewer options and less professional leverage.

But national or regional unemployment rates for the United States, Texas, or Dallas — aren't very specific to the *job* you do; they just show you what's going on with a certain geographic area.

But fortunately we can dig deeper than this.

There is sector job data released in monthly reports, and there is also other industry data that offers insights into the potential for certain jobs, like monthly reports on auto sales, retail sales, and construction.

In fact, the best predictor of job activity in an individual sector will usually be sector-specific data related to sales levels or service activity.

Like if auto sales are hot, then more auto salespeople are likely to be hired. After all, hot sectors need people to work in them.

Of course, if your sector is *not* hot, then you need to be looking around. A solid regional job market will improve your professional job chances. Like if the job market is hot in Chicago and you live in Chicago.

That's good from a regional standpoint. And if your sector is slow, you also want to be watching data for other sectors for a potential new job.

If you work in a department store, and your professional options narrow due to increased e-commerce, you might consider changing your career field to healthcare. If you want some more information on this, you might like to check out BLS resources like their forecasts of the fastest-growing occupations in the United States through 2026.

As you can see in Figure 5-1, there are three columns: the percent growth expected, the number of jobs (in thousands) expected to be created, and the median annual wages of these jobs.

The percent of new jobs, number of new jobs, and pay of new jobs are not all the same. Personal care aides, home health aides, and software developers have the greatest number of total jobs created. But software developer wages are almost five times higher than the other two. It's worth it to dig into this kind of data as you consider career options.

And it's also good to watch economic data releases along with these kinds of data.

For example, if you're watching monthly sector reports, and you see sharp increases in home sales, it may make you think about the fact that people are behind those increases in sales — and there may be growing job opportunities in real estate.

Or maybe you have been watching monthly jobs reports and the trend of rising healthcare jobs inspires you to think about the evergreen needs for healthcare jobs in the U.S. economy for years to come.

This makes watching the jobs reports and sector reports directly related to your profession — and other professions you would consider working in — important data to watch.

Figure 5-1: Fastest-Growing U.S. Occupations[1]

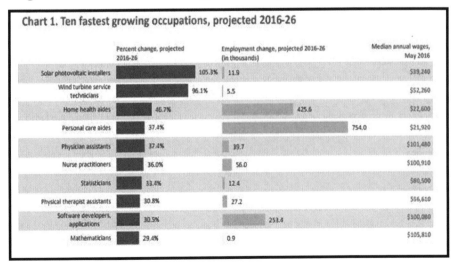

How does the activity data look for your profession and industry?

Are there other sectors with stronger growth or more opportunities for employment and advancement?

What about your region? Are a ton of unemployed people in your area keeping wages low?

Looking at the right economic data can help you make important decisions about your future. Some sector and employment report links are in the Data Appendix.

CHAPTER 6

IMPACTS ON SECTORS

Economic indicators are like dominoes.

One piece of data can impact another, which impacts another, and another, and so on.

Boom. Boom. Boom.

Each economic indicator is at the start of an economic domino effect.

As the dynamics in one report ripple through related industries, other dominoes rise and fall. This is where the real value of understanding economic indicators can be found.

Business leaders, investors, and employees need to know how companies and sectors are performing, so let's talk about how economic indicators impact them.

And we will talk about first order, second order, and third order impacts. The economic ripple effect that one data point can have on other industries may seem at first glance to be somewhat unrelated.

Look at it this way: If I push on a domino and it falls, that's the first order of business — the first economic impact. It's direct, it's in the same industry as the indicator, and it's clear: Retail sales data logically should directly impact retail companies.

It's pretty normal that a good retail sales report could send the stock price of Target or Walmart higher.

When that domino falls, it pushes another domino down (that's the second order). Like the rise in business activity or the rise in the stock price of some of the companies that supply the bedding or clothing to Target and Walmart.

When that second domino falls on a third, that's the third order impact.

That's like seeing the price of cotton rise because of expected strong bedding and clothing demand.

And it's the same thing with other economic indicators.

Each economic report has implications for a number of different sectors in the economy.

If you work in real estate and housing permits fall, which is the number of permits filed to build new homes, it means that fewer new homes are being planned — and fewer new homes will be built and fewer new homes will be sold. This is a first-order impact — the first domino to fall.

When data like that slows, people in real estate are the first to know, because they will be the first to feel it.

But there are other ripple effects — other dominoes that will be impacted by this data.

As a second-order impact, if home sales slow sharply, you won't need as many new refrigerators or washing machines for new homes, so you could see Bosch or Kenmore lower their production forecasts, homebuilders like D.R. Horton could slow their hiring, and even lumber companies like Weyerhaeuser could defer some logging activities.

As you can see, bad housing data could cause other related industries to slow down.

For jobs, this second-order impact of lowered appliance production and slowed construction hiring often means a hiring freeze or layoffs.

There could also be a slowdown in equipment purchases and other business investments by companies in those sectors.

Of course, there are still third-order impacts! If you sell aluminum like Alcoa to an appliance manufacturer like GE, and GE reduces its orders of appliances, you could see a slowdown in your business as well.

And another third-order impact would be on the companies like Caterpillar that sell logging equipment to that lumber company... those businesses could also slow.

To find economic indicators that matter most for your company, ask yourself:
— What industries does your company serve?
— Are there customers of your customers?
— If so, is there economic data available for health of the very last customer — the end user of what you do? Like auto sales, home sales, retail sales?

Find those indicators that reflect the health of the end user, and latch on to them.

For business planning, personal career planning, and for investing, you need to follow the money to the very last dollar.

CHAPTER 7

IMPACTS ON INVESTMENTS

At 8:30 a.m. Eastern Time on what is usually the first Friday of the month, the U.S. Bureau of Labor Statistics releases the employment report.

Every month for over 15 years, I have sat glued to my computer, with business TV running in the background, waiting for this report, because this is the most important monthly piece of data for the U.S. economy — and it often causes the biggest movements in financial markets in any given month.

In banks and on trading desks, this day is known as "jobs day."

When the numbers are good, people on trading desks usually cheer. When it's bad, there are usually a lot of loud grunts, groans, screams — and maybe even a couple of broken desk phones.

The U.S. jobs report impacts the dollar, equity markets, interest rates, bond prices, and precious metals prices. It can even impact industrial commodities, like aluminum, copper, and oil.

Macroeconomic Impacts Across Markets

If you've invested in any of a wide range of financial markets, negative macroeconomic reports — like a bad jobs report — can adversely impact your entire investment portfolio.

And the jobs report isn't the only piece of data that can significantly impact financial markets — and your investments.

There are a number of economic reports that offer important insights into the health of the economy. And if the economy isn't feeling well, your investment portfolio might not be either.

Economic indicators impact what happens to the prices of the stocks you own, your mutual funds, your ETFs, and the prices of the bonds you own.

A good jobs report or a strong report of GDP (which is a measure of national growth and stands for gross domestic product) can impact a lot of investments at once. Stock prices go up, and you see traders on the floor of the New York Stock Exchange cheering. A lot of people — myself included — often trade around economic indicators.

Have you ever heard the phrase "there's a lot of red on the screen" or "there's a lot of green on the screen?"

These are two things that financial professionals and traders say, because when an investment falls, it shows up as red on trading platforms. When an investment goes up, it shows up as green. They do this on Bloomberg TV, CNBC, and Fox Business.

When an important national report is bad, like if GDP falls and shows an economy is in recession, or a jobs report shows unemployment rising sharply, the result is that there is often "a lot of red on the screen," because a lot of investments lose value.

Conversely, when an important national report is good — like strong growth in GDP or a sharp drop in the unemployment rate — there is often "a lot of green on the screen," because a lot of investments have increased their value.

Bottom line: Economic indicators impact your wealth, your income, and your retirement savings.

And this happens in economies around the world.

But not every report will impact every market.

If you have investments in Canada, Germany, and Brazil, you might see a lot of red on the screen in one economy, but the hope is that your risk is diversified in case any single economy sees a slowdown in GDP or a rise in unemployment.

Think about the investments you have. Are you exposed to just one economy? If so, one bad economic report could hurt every financial investment you own.

I've included a list of economic indicator reports in the Data Appendix along with a link to the World Economic Outlook database from the International Monetary Fund, or IMF, so you know where to find important data from a number of different economies.

Impacts on Sector Investments

Are you one of the 150 million Americans who owns stocks?

If you are, then you need to know how the sectors of your investments are going to perform and the right economic sector data — like housing, auto, and energy reports — that can help you get there! And there are a number of ways that economic indicators for certain sectors can impact your investments.

While national economic data, like inflation and unemployment, are important for investments in an entire economy, sector data are critical for investments in sectors related to — or impacted by — the data.

Some of the most important sector reports are for retail sales, real estate, energy, and agriculture. These can also have big impacts on your investments. If a monthly retail sales report is good, you could see the stock prices of department stores — like Target, Walmart, and Amazon — rise sharply. And this could send investments for the entire retail sector higher.

You can also see this kind of market impact on companies and investments related to commodities in weekly oil and gas inventory reports. Understandably, those reports can move commodity prices — and energy investments.

If you own Exxon stock (or if Exxon stock is in a basket of energy stocks or ETF you own) and oil prices collapse, that might be something you would want to know, because oil price movements are highly correlated with the prices of oil and gas companies — and your stock would be likely to lose value.

Beyond regularly scheduled weekly indicators, other economic reports can also move markets significantly.

For example, an annual outlook that includes long-term forecasts of the number of electric vehicles in the United States can impact everything from the price of stock of a company that specializes in electric vehicles, like Tesla, to the bond price of a coal producer like Peabody. And it can impact the price of oil and impact stock prices of oil and gas producers like BP or Shell.

There are also similar risks for agricultural prices. Regular planting reports offer insight into the acreage of planted crops like corn, wheat, and soy. These impact grain prices — and they can impact companies that sell farming equipment, like John Deere or Caterpillar, as well as companies that manufacture cereal, like General Mills. If you have investments in these companies, the planting report could be very important in making decisions about how to manage your financial investment portfolio.

As you can see, sector data are important for investments.

Think about the investments you have. What markets are important for them? Is there a sector indicator relevant for them, like new home sales, retail sales, or service sector activity? Or maybe energy and agricultural data are critical?

There are regular economic indicator reports for all of these, and if you want to stay on top of your investments, you would be wise to watch these reports closely.

Leading Economic Data

CHAPTER 8

GLOBAL PURCHASING MANAGER INDICES

The most important forward-looking economic indicators are purchasing manager indices (PMIs), which are surveys of purchasing managers at manufacturing firms. These are good data points for assessing growth because they are easy to understand, and they show in real time what purchasing managers — the people who buy raw materials and inputs at factories — are doing.

PMIs are easy to understand because the breakeven level for the indices is 50. In other words, if purchasing managers are buying more on a monthly basis, a PMI will be above 50, which is indicative of increased production runs for finished goods — and is a precondition for growth.

Readings below 50, however, are indicative of monthly contractions. PMIs are as close to real time as you can get for significant economic data. This is because PMIs are typically released in the first week of the month, following the month in which the data were collected.

The most important manufacturing purchasing manager indices are the U.S. ISM Manufacturing Index, the Chinese Caixin Manufacturing PMI, and the Eurozone Manufacturing PMI. Also important are the German Ifo and the U.S. ISM Non-Manufacturing PMI.

These PMIs and other leading economic indicators are subjects of the following chapters. Figure 8-1 shows the three critical PMIs — the Chinese Caixin, Eurozone Manufacturing PMI, and the U.S. ISM Manufacturing Index.

Equally important to the health of the global economy and global manufacturing is the sum of these three PMIs.

Figure 8-1: Three Critical PMIs[1]

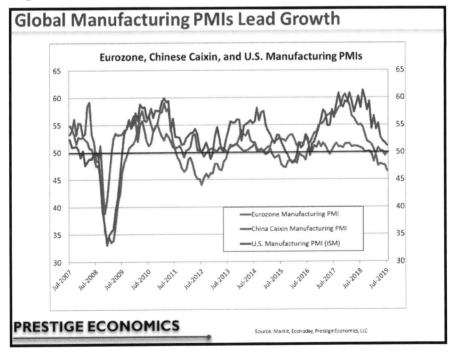

Since a breakeven level for each index is 50, the sum breakeven for the three data series is 150.

In Figure 8-2, you can see the sum of these three PMIs. When they are strong, and well above the 150 breakeven level, it is bullish for industrial commodity markets and emerging market equities.

But when the PMI sum is below 150, it is bearish for industrial commodity demand and prices, like oil prices and industrial metals prices.

Figure 8-2: Sum of Three Critical PMIs[2]

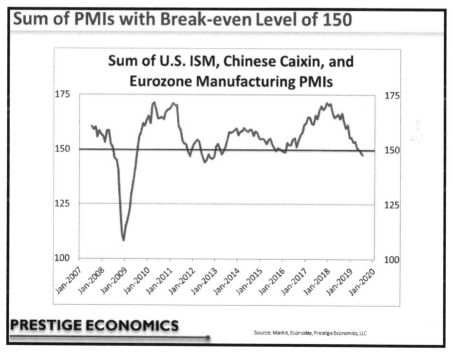

CHAPTER 9

ISM MANUFACTURING INDEX

I give dozens of speeches every year.

And sometimes a group will tell me I can only use one graph.

They only want me to talk about one data point.

When that happens, I talk about the U.S. ISM Manufacturing Index, a survey of 300 manufacturing firms, collected by the Institute for Supply Management.

It is the single most important forward-looking piece of data for the U.S. economy.

It's critical for jobs, the stock market, and economic growth. And by that, I mean it is the best predictor of whether the U.S. economy is expanding, or whether it is at risk of a slowdown or recession.

So, why is the ISM Manufacturing Index so important?

After all manufacturing is a relatively small part — only around 11 or 12 percent — of U.S. economy. And it represents less than 9 percent of all U.S. jobs.

But manufacturing is a capital-intensive part of the economy, which means that it requires a lot of money to run manufacturing businesses.

And if manufacturing slows, it usually indicates that credit is tightening up, and business won't invest money to grow, and the economy is likely to slow down, and jobs could evaporate.

But if manufacturing is expanding, it is likely to lead the economy to higher levels of growth.

That's why manufacturing matters as a leading indicator for the overall economy.

Purchasing Managers
As for purchasing managers, they are a bellwether for manufacturing, because purchasing managers are the people who actually buy stuff to manufacture finished goods.

Before you get a finished car, you need to buy the metal and plastic and parts that go into it. So, a purchasing manager at an auto manufacturing firm (for example) purchases materials to build a car.

That purchasing manager might buy tires, hubcaps, bumpers, or windshield wipers.

And why would the purchasing manager buy these items? It would be because there are car orders that need to be filled.

And when that car is finished, it will be counted as part of GDP — it will be counted as part of economic growth.

More cars of course mean more GDP, while less cars could mean less GDP.

If that automotive purchasing manager is buying more materials, that means the company probably has more orders for new cars.

If the purchasing manager is buying less, the company probably has fewer orders.

The ISM Manufacturing Index records the responses of purchasing managers across the U.S. economy in a way that reflects their current buying activity, which is a leading predictor of future completed orders and GDP.

When the ISM is below 50, purchasing managers are buying less across the entire economy from one month to the next.

This means that fewer new orders will be filled, growth is poised to slow, and the economy could fall into recession, with job losses to accompany it.

If the ISM is above 50, it means that purchasing managers in the United States broadly are seeing an expansion in their buying activity.

They are buying more — this means that more new orders will be filled, growth is poised to rise, and the economy is likely to grow.

And when the ISM is at 50, purchasing managers are buying the same amount of goods from one month to the next. Of course, this isn't great either, since most economies tend to grow over time.

For example, Figure 9-1 shows the ISM Manufacturing Index.

You can see it fall below 50 during the Great Recession — and even at the end of 2015 and in early 2016, when business investment was very weak.

Figure 9-1: U.S. ISM Manufacturing Index[1]

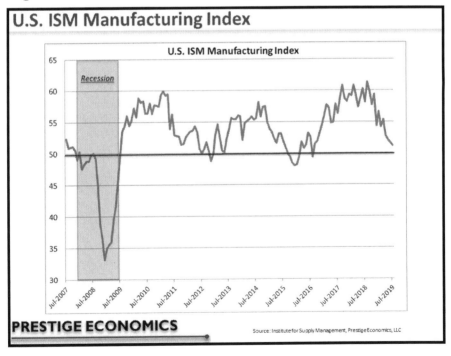

At that time, the U.S. economy was at risk of a recession, but the ISM rebounded in 2016, and the overall economy strengthened, avoiding a potential downturn, stock market crash, and job losses.

Whenever this index again falls below 50, it would represent risks of a slowdown in business investment, of a slowing economy, and of coming jobs losses and recession.

If you care about the health of the U.S. economy — job growth, economic growth, and equity markets, I would encourage you to watch the ISM Manufacturing Index at the beginning of every month.

The data is on the ISM website here:
https://www.instituteforsupplymanagement.org

It's a report I follow closely. And I encourage you to do the same.

CHAPTER 10

ISM NON-MANUFACTURING INDEX

The U.S. is a service economy.

And probably in a bigger way than you think.

When I say services, many people think of fast food.

This is because when politicians sometimes talk about low-quality service jobs they often use fast food restaurant jobs as an example.

But services represent almost 80 percent of the economy. That includes accounting, legal, and financial services, not just fast food, massage therapy, and manicure services.

And at 80 percent of the economy, an indicator of service sector activity is naturally an important way to track growth for the majority of the U.S. economy. And the Institute for Supply Management — or ISM — Non-Manufacturing Index is the #1 indicator of service sector activity in the United States.

The ISM Non-Manufacturing Index report includes a survey of purchasing managers from over 400 companies about their monthly business activities.

The main number in this report is called a Purchasing Manager Index — or a PMI. And the breakeven level for the PMI is 50.

A PMI above 50 means that the non-manufacturing part of the economy — the 80 percent of the U.S. economy in services — is expanding and growing. And when 80 percent of your economy is growing, this is good for jobs, the stock market, and national wealth.

Believe me, the stocks in your retirement account like it when the ISM Non-Manufacturing Index is above 50.

So, what's in this important survey?

This PMI includes responses from non-manufacturing companies that participate in the survey, including banks, real estate firms, transportation and other industries that are not in manufacturing.

It's pretty clear when you talk about manufacturing what those companies are buying. Auto manufacturers buy car parts and metals. Toy companies buy plastic and cotton. And furniture companies buy wood and glass.

For non-manufacturing companies, this is often a bit less obvious.

Some of the things these companies purchase include paper for printing, office supplies, and various services — like legal and IT.

When the ISM Non-Manufacturing Index is above 50, it's good for the economy — and most investments that depend on positive economic growth. But when the ISM Non-Manufacturing Index is below 50, that's bad.

Because when that happens, it means that 80 percent of the U.S. economy is contracting.

Fortunately, the ISM Non-Manufacturing Index is usually above 50, as can be seen in Figure 10-1.

Figure 10-1: U.S. ISM Non-Manufacturing Index[1]

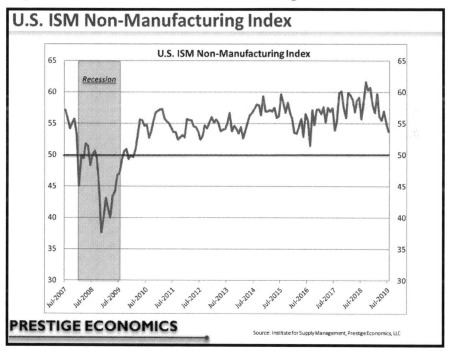

CHAPTER 11

CHINESE CAIXIN MANUFACTURING PMI

China is the second-largest economy in the world. And it's the biggest manufacturing economy in the world.

In fact, manufacturing is almost a quarter of the Chinese economy.

It's a core reason why manufacturing in China is critical for global manufacturing, global growth, and global commodity market demand — and prices.

As in the United States, where the ISM Manufacturing Index is critical, the Chinese Caixin Manufacturing PMI is critical.

In fact, there are two Chinese PMIs: a private PMI and a government PMI. Given questions of validity that often accompany Chinese government data, the Caixin Manufacturing PMI is one of the few consistently reliable reports since it is privately compiled.

Based on the Chinese Caixin Manufacturing PMI, there was a Chinese manufacturing recession that lasted from December 2014 until June 2016. The contraction in Chinese manufacturing resulted in a massive softening in global commodity markets, which is why during that time industrial metals prices came under sharp pressure, as did oil prices.

But throughout 2018 and in 2019, the Chinese Caixin weakened — and it has contracted in some recent months. The absolute level of the index has also been lower than the ISM Manufacturing Index. Chinese Caixin PMI weakness can be seen in Figure 11-1.

Figure 11-1: Chinese Caixin Manufacturing PMI[1]

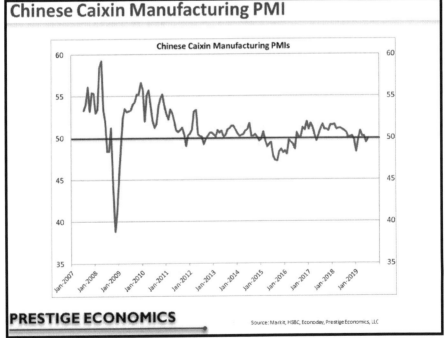

The weakness is indicative of downside risks to global growth and manufacturing. And as in the last Chinese manufacturing recession, the recent weakness in the Chinese Caixin Manufacturing PMI has again weighed on industrial metals prices and oil prices.

Recent Chinese weakness has been engendered in no small part by the U.S.-China trade war. And the prospects for trade relations between the United States and China will be critical for the future of Chinese manufacturing.

I've been writing about commodity markets — and forecasting commodity prices — for over 15 years. And the Chinese Caixin is currently the most critical indicator for those markets.

CHAPTER 12

EUROZONE MANUFACTURING PMI

The Eurozone is one of the three biggest economies in the world, along with the United States and China.

And the Eurozone is made up of more than a dozen countries that use the euro and whose central bank policy is set by the European Central Bank in Frankfurt, Germany.

And the most important leading economic indicator that offers insight into the future growth, employment, and business activity in Europe is the Eurozone Manufacturing Purchasing Manager Index — or PMI.

Like the U.S. ISM and the Chinese Caixin, the Eurozone Manufacturing PMI is released at the beginning of every month, and it conveys survey results about manufacturing activity from the prior month.

Like other purchasing manager indices, this survey has a breakeven level of 50.

If it's above 50, Eurozone manufacturing is expanding. If it is below 50 Eurozone manufacturing is contracting.

Manufacturing is important because it leads economic growth, and even if the index is above 50, sharp drops can indicate that the Eurozone economy is about to slow.

And for the average person?

If you have investments in Europe or a business that buys or sells goods in Europe, or if you're planning your next vacation to Paris or Rome, you should care about the health of the Eurozone economy, because the level of the euro will impact your investments, the cost to business in Europe, and the exchange rates that will impact the cost of your Parisian baguettes and pizza in Rome.

Recent dynamics in the Eurozone Manufacturing PMI can be seen in Figure 12-1.

As the European Central Bank reduced its balance sheet between mid-2012 and late 2014, growth in the Eurozone began to slow, and the prospects of a third recession were high. With the implementation of an ECB quantitative easing program at the beginning of 2015, a third recession was averted.

The Eurozone strengthened further, with its manufacturing PMI rising to a record all-time high in December 2017. But the PMI slowed sharply in 2018 and contracted in 2019. This underscores downside risks to Eurozone growth in 2019.

Eurozone manufacturing and growth experienced a double-dip recession in the wake of the European sovereign debt crisis. And the current data, with the PMI below 50, indicate that there is currently a recession in Eurozone manufacturing, with significant risks of an overall recession in the Eurozone economy imminently.

While the Eurozone Manufacturing PMI is currently below 50, it will be above 50 again. And when it rises, that will be indicative of an expanding Eurozone economy.

It's why this is a critical economic indicator to watch for the future of the Eurozone economy, the strength of the euro, and Eurozone investments.

Figure 12-1: Eurozone Manufacturing PMI[1]

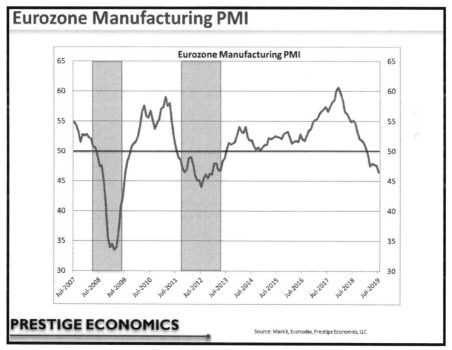

CHAPTER 13

GERMAN IFO

While the most important leading economic indicator of Eurozone growth is the Eurozone Manufacturing PMI, another critical leading indicator is the German Ifo.

The German Ifo is named for the organization that produces the index, the Institut für Wirtschaftsforschung, which compiles the data and translates to the institute for economic research.

While the Eurozone Manufacturing PMI data for each month comes out at the beginning of the next month, the German Ifo comes out during the month for which it is providing activity.

For example, while the June 2018 Eurozone Manufacturing PMI was released on 1 July 2018, the German Ifo was released during the month of June on 25 June 2018.

Economists and analysts are always looking for a better way to predict what will happen to financial markets and the economy.

And the German Ifo is just a little earlier than the Eurozone manufacturing PMI.

Of course, the German economy is the biggest economy in the Eurozone. It represents over 20 percent, or one-fifth, of the Eurozone economy. But it is by no means the lion's share. Nevertheless, this German indicator is hotly watched and one of the most important in Europe.

The German Ifo does not have a breakeven level, but it includes three main numbers:

- An assessment of the *current business situation.*
- A six-month ahead *outlook.*
- An overall *economic sentiment* number, which is an average of the other two series.

It's that average — the economic sentiment number — that is quoted in the mainstream media. And it's the number investors, strategists, and analysts focus on.

A strong Ifo — especially a strong trend — can be bullish for the Euro and positive for European equities.

But the impact isn't always just limited to Europe.

Strength in the Ifo can support equities in a way that has a positive ripple through global equity markets.

But, conversely, a very weak report can also have contagion risks across global markets.

After all, a weak German Ifo can send European markets lower, and this can impact the U.S. markets, which can in turn negatively impact Asian markets.

In general, if you only watch two data points out of Europe to give you indication about Eurozone growth, they should be the Eurozone Manufacturing PMI and the German Ifo.

CHAPTER 14

CONSUMER CONFIDENCE

About 70 percent of the U.S. economy is driven by personal consumption. And this includes the stuff that regular people like you and I buy, including clothes, cars, and food.

This makes the U.S. economy less susceptible to recessions as long as people have jobs and they are spending money.

And, of course, we're not going to go on too many shopping sprees if we don't feel very confident about the economy.

In fact, if I'm nervous about the economy, I tend to buy fewer things. I may postpone buying a new car or sofa, and I might even start buying cheaper wine to bring to friend's birthday parties.

The truth is that if people are confident about the economy, they will spend money. And if they aren't, they won't!

This is why the monthly Consumer Confidence Index from The Conference Board is an important economic indicator: It shows how confident American consumers are.

And that implication of confidence means a lot for financial markets. Strong confidence numbers are good for most stock prices, but weak confidence numbers are bad for the economy and equity markets.

The Nielson Company has been operating the survey for The Conference Board as a random sampling designed to reflect confidence across the American economy. This is the same Nielson that produces ratings for TV shows.

That's not to say that consumer confidence is anything like the TV shows *Game of Thrones* or *The Walking Dead*.

But consumer confidence can be a blockbuster for financial markets!

Retail stocks, auto manufacturers, and other companies that sell goods — and services — directly to consumers are most exposed to this kind of report, both on the upside and the downside.

The Consumer Confidence Index number you might read about in *USA Today*, hear about on NPR, or see on Bloomberg Television is an average of the responses to five questions: Two questions are about the present situation and three are about future expectations.

This makes sense, because how confident you feel about the economy is likely a mix of how you are doing now — and how you think you'll be doing in the future.

These five questions create three indices:

- Total *Consumer Confidence Index*, which is an average of all five questions
- *Present Situation Index*, which is the average of two present questions
- *Future Expectations Index*, which is the average of three future questions

The two questions in the Present Situation Index basically ask how you feel about current business. Is it better, worse, or unchanged from last month?

And there's a similar question about present employment conditions.

The three questions in the Future Situation Index ask something like: How has your opinion of the economy in six months changed? Is it better, worse, or unchanged since last month?

The other two future questions are similar, and they address employment and family income six months in the future.

The total consumer confidence number offers a view of confidence overall, while the present situation and future expectations indices offer a chance to make comparisons that can have implications for the economy, jobs, and investments.

Let me give you a couple examples:

In a recession, the current index might be very low — like 85 — but the expectations index could be higher, like 95 or 100. This would be a good sign that the recession might soon end, since the outlook for the future is better than the present.

On the flipside, if the current number is high — like 120 — but the expectations number is lower — like 100 — that could be a bad sign that the economy is likely to slow, because people are less confident about the future than the present.

Those comparisons between the present and the future are important.

But the most important number is the overall Consumer Confidence Index, and how that changes on a monthly basis is the most important factor for financial markets.

After all, as every financial analyst knows, the two biggest drivers of financial markets are fear and greed.

But if consumers feel fear, it will be reflected in lower spending, lower growth, and, very likely, lower stock prices.

So, if you want to know what data might lead job creation in retail, the stock prices of the retail sector as a whole, and equity markets overall, consumer confidence is a critical indicator to watch.

Because indicators like The Conference Board's Consumer Confidence offer a glimpse into the mindset of consumers — the #1 driving force of the entire U.S. economy.

CHAPTER 15

LEADING ECONOMIC INDICATORS

A friend of mine's email signature has the quote "I just want tomorrow's *Wall Street Journal* today."

In other words, he wants to be able to know the economic and financial market future before it happens. And many people feel this way, because the economy impacts their jobs and investments.

As I mentioned there are three kinds of economic indicators back in Chapter 3. Economic indicators that offer a glimpse into the future are called leading economic indicators, because they lead economic growth.

Those reflecting the present are called coincident economic indicators because the data they include best coincides with current economic activities.

And there are economic indicators that show the past, called lagging economic indicators because they lag behind the actual dynamics in the economy.

In short, if you want to feel like you're reading tomorrow's *WSJ* today, you want to be watching leading economic indicators closely.

And there is even a report that focuses on these indicators, called The Leading Economic Indicator Index (LEI), which is produced by the organization The Conference Board.

This Leading Economic Index, often called the LEI, is a useful tool, because it includes 10 different components. Think of it as a forward-looking spicy data goulash. These 10 components for the United States are related to a number of key topics.

There are two data parts for jobs:
— Average weekly hours, manufacturing
— Average weekly initial claims for unemployment insurance

And there are three data parts for manufacturing orders:
— Manufacturers' new orders, consumer goods and materials
— ISM® Index of New Orders
— Manufacturers' new orders, nondefense capital goods excluding aircraft orders

The LEI also includes data related to housing:
— Housing: Building permits, new private housing units
— Equities: Stock prices, 500 common stocks
— Credit: *Leading Credit Index*™ Interest rate spread, 10-year Treasury bonds less federal funds
— Expected business conditions: Average consumer expectations for business conditions

As you can see, the LEI is a basket of leading data points that are widely known to be — as a whole — a good predictor of future market trading. Which is why one of the main purposes of the LEI is to "signal peaks and troughs in the business cycle."

Most people who trade actively in markets can trade a trend — like when the markets are going up or going down. This is especially true for technical traders, but the biggest questions in trading, risk, and strategy usually are: Where are the peaks? Where are the troughs?

In other words, how do I know that I've made all the money I'm going to make and it's time to sell? And how do I know when it's time to buy again?

In sum, bottoms and tops are tougher to identify, but that's what the LEI does. And as financial traders are known for saying, "All you get when you pick bottoms are stinky fingers."

While traders may be moving money around this indicator, economists often bet something bigger on the LEI: their reputations.

When on recession watch, economists look to the LEI to confirm or refute their concerns about the economy.

I remember speaking to one economist in early 2016, when U.S. business investment was in recession — and other economic indicators were pointing to a recession as well.

But he wasn't ready to call an imminent recession just yet, because the LEI hadn't weakened enough. In the end, he was right, and it was because he was watching the LEI.

In 2018, as equity markets were hitting all-time highs and consumer confidence returned to levels not seen since 2000, the LEI was still being watched closely for topping.

For the average person — like you and me — the LEI is important because if it falls, your investments could tank as well — and your job may be at risk.

The LEI is critical, because it isn't just focused on one market, like autos or housing.

The LEI is important for the entire economy, which means that if it falls and signals a recession, companies across the economy could take a hit:
— Amazon and Caterpillar
— Disney and Ford
— Apple and Exxon

And many other companies in the economy.

No matter where you are investing in the U.S. economy, you are likely exposed to a major drop in the LEI.

Of course, continued and persistent rises in LEI are likely to be positive for your investments across the U.S. economy.

For overall activity — especially at those important bottoms and tops of growth — the LEI is a critical indicator to watch.

The Importance of Policy

CHAPTER 16

QUARTERLY IMF REPORTS

The International Monetary Fund has 189 member countries — almost every country in the world. So, it makes sense that the IMF has its finger on the pulse of global economic growth.

It's also the reason why the IMF forecasts of global growth, which are produced quarterly, are very important for expectations about the future health of the economy — and why they are important for commodity prices and global stock markets.

Plus, emerging markets like Turkey, Brazil, India, and China are especially dependent on the rate of growth for the global economy. After all, they are providers of critical manufactured goods and raw materials to the global economy.

In years with a good pace of global growth, emerging markets are likely to have boom years, while a slower pace of global growth usually has outsized negative impacts on emerging markets.

The International Monetary Fund is a leading nongovernmental organization — or NGO — that facilitates international trade, promotes employment and sustainable economic growth, and helps to reduce global poverty. So naturally, the growth outlook is very important for its mission.

The IMF growth forecasts are released every quarter, and they include forecasts for the coming two years. This two-year outlook is watched closely because it's a reasonable amount of time in the future for investors and business leaders to make plans based on the growth outlook. When you get past two years, it's a lot tougher to forecast the economic outlook.

Let's take a look at the IMF forecasts from the World Economic Outlook (WEO) recent report. This data can be found on the IMF website section for the World Economic Outlook publications at **http://www.imf.org/en/publications/weo**

Once you're there, just scroll down to the most recent World Economic Outlook report or update. This report includes a table of both recent historical rates of GDP growth as well as GDP growth rate forecasts.

This includes forecasts for
- The Global Economy
- Advanced Economies
- Emerging Market Economies
- Individual Economies

You can see what part of the table looks like in Figure 16-1.

Historical GDP growth rates are typically in the left-most columns, while the forecasts for the next two years are typically shown in columns to the right. There are also usually other columns further to the right that show how the IMF forecasts have changed compared to the previous forecast report.

Figure 16-1: IMF GDP Forecasts[1]

Latest *World Economic Outlook* growth projections (percent change)		Projections	
	2018	2019	2020
World Output	**3.6**	**3.2**	**3.5**
Advanced Economies	**2.2**	**1.9**	**1.7**
United States	2.9	2.6	1.9
Euro Area	1.9	1.3	1.6
Germany	1.4	0.7	1.7
France	1.7	1.3	1.4
Italy	0.9	0.1	0.8
Spain	2.6	2.3	1.9
Japan	0.8	0.9	0.4
United Kingdom	1.4	1.3	1.4
Canada	1.9	1.5	1.9
Other Advanced Economies	2.6	2.1	2.4
Emerging Market and Developing Economies	**4.5**	**4.1**	**4.7**
Commonwealth of Independent States	2.7	1.9	2.4
Russia	2.3	1.2	1.9
Excluding Russia	3.9	3.5	3.7
Emerging and Developing Asia	6.4	6.2	6.2
China	6.6	6.2	6.0
India	6.8	7.0	7.2
ASEAN-5	5.2	5.0	5.1
Emerging and Developing Europe	3.6	1.0	2.3
Latin America and the Caribbean	1.0	0.6	2.3
Brazil	1.1	0.8	2.4
Mexico	2.0	0.9	1.9
Middle East, North Africa, Afghanistan, and Pakistan	1.6	1.0	3.0
Saudi Arabia	2.2	1.9	3.0
Sub-Saharan Africa	3.1	3.4	3.6
Nigeria	1.9	2.3	2.6
South Africa	0.8	0.7	1.1
Low-Income Developing Countries	4.9	4.9	5.1
Source: IMF, *World Economic Outlook Update*, July 2019.			

The most important thing to know about the total global growth rate is that 3 percent is very much a breakeven level.

While 3 percent GDP growth sounds great for an advanced economy like the United States or the Eurozone, it's actually a rate that is only roughly in line with global population growth.

So 3 percent global GDP growth is actually rather disappointing.

This means that the global economy should automatically generate an increase of 3 percent in global GDP in any given year, just because there are 3 percent more people on planet earth.

For this reason, a 3 percent forecast is not good, and a global growth rate below 3 percent is bad. It means that capital and technology did not contribute to additional global growth.

In general, global GDP growth above 3.6 percent is likely to be good for equity markets, and its likely to send equity markets higher.

I would offer one caveat as you weigh the importance of the IMF global growth forecasts: They are still just forecasts, and they are often revised lower or higher as economic dynamics change.

There is also one more pro tip to be aware of: There's a press conference every quarter when the IMF releases these forecasts, and you can even send in questions during the live broadcast.

I watch the IMF growth forecasts every quarter.

It's one of the most important things I do, because these forecasts can tell you where the global economy is going. That's important data for most industries and investments.

And it is absolutely critical for industrial metals prices, oil prices, and other global industrial commodities. Combined with PMI and other leading economic reports, the IMF growth forecasts are some of the most important global market-moving data.

CHAPTER 17

OPEC DECISIONS

When politicians, oil analysts, and regular consumers talks about oil prices, they talk about OPEC — the Organization of the Petroleum Exporting Countries.

I have been going to OPEC meetings for about 15 years.

I've even brought my mother with me to several of them. But OPEC meetings are not just a trip you bring your mom on.

They impact oil prices.

As of mid-2019, OPEC has 14 member countries, including Saudi Arabia, Iraq, Iran, Libya, Venezuela, and a number of others.

Plus, beginning in December 2017, OPEC has also been collaborating with additional non-OPEC members, including Russia, Mexico, and a host of others.

OPEC is often branded as a cartel by politicians and economists, but its members do not always agree, and they often act independently of each other. In fact, I think of OPEC more as the central bank of oil.

Plus, OPEC members do not have a monopoly on global oil production. In fact, OPEC member countries produced over 30 million barrels per day of crude oil in mid-2019 — or about one-third of global crude oil supplies.

In other words, even though OPEC members control a lot of oil production, they aren't a monopoly, and they don't act as an effective cartel.

OPEC does not directly set oil prices.

OPEC targets global oil inventories and global oil production to keep oil prices that are high enough to be profitable but not high enough to financially justify abandoning oil as the main source of transportation energy.

And this policy has worked relatively well over the years.

So, how does OPEC do this?

OPEC usually meets twice a year in full formal meetings.

These used to alternate between the OPEC world headquarters in Vienna, Austria, and some of the member countries.

Now, however, OPEC tends to be in Vienna almost all the time.

These meetings are very similar to corporate executive roundtables. The ministers of member countries flock to Vienna and meet in a large room, where they share their thoughts behind closed doors and try to set policies that will satisfy the entire group.

Oil prices impact what you pay at the pump, your company's expenses, and stock prices of oil producers, consumers, and refineries.

If you work for or invest in commodities, energy companies, airlines, refineries, trucking companies, car companies, or shipping firms, OPEC meeting decisions are likely to be a very big deal for you!

The outcome of these meetings could also be important if you live in a city where oil prices are important for the economy, like Houston or Calgary.

Plus, oil prices can drive inflation, which can impact central bank interest rate policy decisions. It's why, in some ways, OPEC is a central bank that can drive the policies of other central banks.

This is why OPEC meetings are some of the hottest, most frenzied media events of the year. OPEC decisions impact energy prices and stock prices of energy companies. Plus, they can impact inflation expectations and interest rates.

CHAPTER 18

FISCAL POLICY

Just like people, governments have to manage their finances.

And whether you think a government is making smart or dumb budget decisions, these activities all fall under the term *fiscal policy*. This is as true in the United States as it is in India, France, and Brazil.

This overarching term really has to do with how a government taxes its citizens and businesses, how it spends that money, and how it manages its debts.

After all, not all governments live within their means. In fact, very few do, which is why fiscal policy also includes how a government raises debt if it cannot afford what is being spent — and how a government manages the interest on its debt — or repays its debts.

All of these policies together are fiscal policy, and they impact interest rates, tax rates — and ultimately — growth rates.

Fiscal policy is important in an economy, because the biggest business in most countries is usually the government itself.

For a number of years, U.S. government spending has represented around 18 percent of the entire U.S. economy.

How a government spends its money can impact a lot of different industries. If there is increased spending on infrastructure, like highways and bridges, construction companies could see a boom — as could the companies that make construction equipment and the companies that transport that equipment.

If a country decides to spend more on its military, companies that manufacture aircraft, weapons, and defense systems could see their orders increase — and their company valuations rise.

But the allocation of government spending can be a fickle thing, and in democracies, the parties in power often change with elections.

And those changes of control can also change whether a government spends more money on education or more money on healthcare. So if a government spends more money, that gets added to the growth calculation. This isn't politics; it's just math.

Whether the government spends more on spy planes, schools, highways, or gold-plated toilets, it makes U.S. economic growth, as measured by gross domestic product (otherwise known as GDP), go up.

But there are two key problems:

First, governments don't usually generate revenue on their own. The money the government has needs to come from taxes.

This means that new money isn't necessarily being created — it might just be moved around, from taxpayers to the government and then somewhere else. And that money may have a more or less positive impact on growth than if the money had been just left in the private sector.

It depends a lot on how and where the money is spent. And spending can be driven by social priorities, for which a clear-cut return on investment is tougher to nail down.

Tax cuts on business equipment usually incentivize companies to buy more equipment, like trucks, computers, or industrial machinery.

Tax increases on payroll taxes may discourage employers from hiring people — and they might *incentivize* and encourage companies to buy more robots or automated solutions.

The second problem is that governments sometimes (or rather often) spend money they don't have, which creates debt.

This is pretty cool to boost your GDP, but if a government spends money it does not have, this can slow future growth, because more debt will lead to higher interest rates.

The level of debt a country has is often shown in two ways: in absolute terms, like U.S. dollars in the United States.

And as a percent of a country's GDP, which is known as the debt-to-GDP ratio.

In Chapter 55, I discuss the long-term trend higher in the U.S. national debt as well as the U.S. debt-to-GDP ratio.

No matter how high or low your country's debt, fiscal policy will impact businesses, consumers, and financial markets.

Check out the World Economic Outlook (WEO) databases of the International Monetary Fund at imf.org for more information on your country's debt level and debt-to-GDP ratio.

I have included a link in the Data Appendix as well.

CHAPTER 19

MONETARY POLICY

Monetary policy is just what it sounds like: a policy for money.

Monetary policy is set by central banks and usually includes interest rates, inflation targets, balance sheet policies, forward guidance, and other activities.

Central banks set important interest rates and they carry — and sometimes expand — their balance sheets. Plus, they also share expectations of future policy, which can also impact the economy.

All of these activities occur under the heading of Monetary Policy.

The most important thing the Fed does is impact interest rates by setting a target for the federal funds rate, which affects the cost of money.

By impacting interest rates that affect the cost of money, the Fed is able to stimulate growth, but it has to strike a careful balance between inflation and growth.

Every central bank has to carefully strike this balance, but it's explicit for the Fed, which has a so-called *dual mandate* — to keep the U.S. economy at full employment and to keep inflation contained near a 2 percent target.

When the U.S. economy is slow or in recession, the Fed cuts these rates, which is a move to loosen monetary policy.

This makes it cheaper for individuals and companies to borrow money, which stimulates the economy and supports economic growth.

Of course, sometimes the economy gets too hot, and inflation becomes the bigger concern.

And when inflation heats up, the Fed usually raises interest rates, which is also called tightening monetary policy. This can indirectly cause business investment to slow, which would cause overall growth to slow — and dampen inflation.

Beyond impacting interest rates, the Fed and other central banks can expand their balance sheets.

You see, central banks keep reserves of their own currency and that of other countries on hand.

The assets they hold are on something called a central bank balance sheet.

And they can increase what they hold, as the Fed did after the Great Recession during 2007-2009, by buying mortgage-backed securities and government Treasuries. This was an extreme measure to lower interest rates and stimulate growth — and it worked.

This process after the Great Recession was called "Quantitative Easing" or QE and you can see in Figure 19-1 how the Fed balance sheet quadrupled, rising from less than $1 trillion before the Great Recession in 2007 to a peak level of just above $4.5 trillion. The Fed subsequently reduced its balance sheet in 2018 and 2019. But if the economy slows, the Fed could increase the balance sheet again.

Figure 19-1: Federal Reserve Balance Sheet[1]

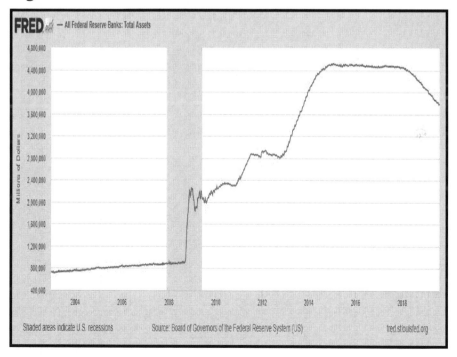

Similar QE programs were implemented in the Eurozone, Japan, and other economies after the GR in order to stimulate growth by lowering interest rates. Central bank balance sheet policy is something I discuss further in Chapter 44.

Beyond interest rate and QE policy, central banks can impact the economy by just talking about their future plans. Sometimes, just talking is enough to impact financial markets and the economy.

Like if the European Central Bank says it is planning to lower rates further, that can actually encourage investment and spending, while talking about raising interest rates can cause a reduction in spending.

This is called forward guidance — talking about policy without actually changing it.

One last thing I need to share is that there are certain animal terms people use when talking about monetary policy.

I'm sure you've heard people talk about being bullish on the stock market (which means they expect it will go up) or being bearish (which means they expect it will go down).

When it comes to the Fed and other central banks, the terms are for the birds.

Literally.

When a central bank is going to make money more expensive and raise interest rates or reduce its balance sheet, this is a tightening policy, and the central bank is said to be *hawkish* when it favors this action.

But when a central bank is going to make money cheaper by lowering rates or expanding its balance sheet, this is looser monetary policy, and the central bank is said to be *dovish* when it favors this action.

These terms hawk and dove can even be used to reference one particular member of a central bank's policy board.

But hawk or dove, you can't think about the economy or interest rates without thinking about monetary policy and central banks.

Employment and Jobs Data

CHAPTER 20

MONTHLY EMPLOYMENT REPORT

Jobs are important.

This is why if you're an investor, trader, or any kind of worker, the most important day of the month is usually the first Friday of the month.

It certainly is for me.

This isn't because I love Fridays and hate my job — I love what do!

It's because the most important economic indicator for all financial markets is usually released on the first Friday of the month.

This report — this economic indicator — is known as the U.S. employment report or more simply "the jobs report." That's what it's called by people on CNBC and Bloomberg Television.

Why is the jobs report so important? Well, that's the easy part.

This report shows the health of the economy in terms of jobs. And everyone cares about jobs — you and me, as well as politicians from both political parties and the central bankers at the Federal Reserve.

This is why the numbers in the jobs report impact foreign exchange rates, bond rates, and stock prices.

There's a lot of information in the jobs report, but there are four big numbers that most directly impact financial markets, job prospects, and expectations of interest rates.

Net Change in Payrolls
First, there's the number of jobs created during the month prior to the release. This is the number with the greatest potential to impact financial markets.

This number is sometimes called non-farm payrolls, because it shows changes in U.S. payrolls across all industries — except agriculture. It sounds weird, but when this data was created, there were a lot more farmers. Plus, agricultural hiring is also very seasonal and could be noisy for the overall jobs data.

Let's look at an example.

The March jobs report will be released at the beginning of April, and it shows the number of net new jobs created in March compared to February.

If the number is 250,000, that means that there were 250,000 more people working in the month of March than in February.

That's good news for the economy, and it can send stock prices higher.

Conversely, if the number is negative 250,000, that means there were 250,000 fewer people working in the month of March than in February. That is very bad news for the economy, and that could send stock prices down sharply.

The depiction of these monthly net changes in U.S. jobs from the monthly employment report is depicted in Figure 20-1.

Figure 20-1: Non-Farm Payrolls[1]

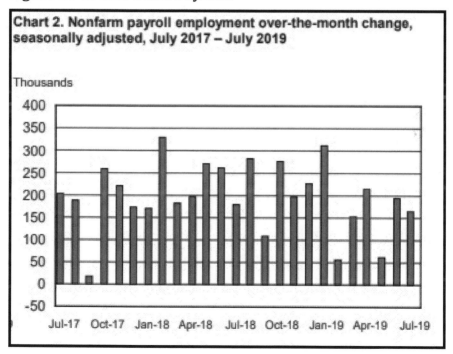

Unemployment Rate

The second big number in the jobs report is the unemployment rate, which shows the percent of people who are part of the labor force who cannot get jobs but want jobs.

This is the number politicians like to talk about. This is an important number on trend, because it tends not to move too much in any given month.

In general, the number of jobs created tends to have a bigger impact on markets. This is especially true, because the unemployment rate also tends to lag economic activity.

Figure 20-2: Unemployment Rate[2]

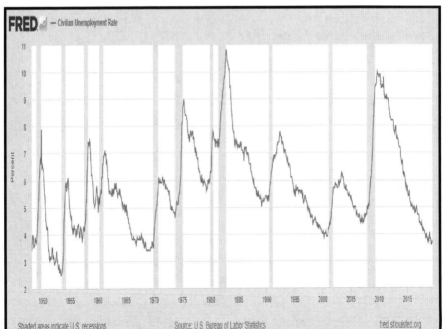

This is why the unemployment rate can rise (which is bad) even after a recession ends (which is good). In fact, this happened in the Great Recession of 2007-2009, which technically ended in June 2009. Meanwhile the unemployment rate kept rising until it peaked at 10.0 percent in October 2009. You can see this dynamic in Figure 20-2.

Labor Force Participation Rates

One important figure that can also impact the unemployment rate is the labor force participation rate. That's the percent of people in the U.S. labor force who either have jobs or are unemployed and looking for jobs. That percentage fell sharply after the Great Recession, as you can see in Figure 20-3.

Figure 20-3: Labor Force Participation Rate[3]

The labor force participation rate dropped at that time and thereafter due to a reduction in job opportunities and a concomitant rise in discouraged workers.

Hourly Earnings

The third big number in the employment report is average hourly earnings, which reflects wage gains — or wage inflation.

This percent shows how much people's average hourly wages are up from the previous year. If this number is up a lot — like 3 percent or more — it can be a big concern for financial markets, because that level of inflation is likely to require the U.S. central bank to raise interest rates.

Figure 20-4: Hourly Earnings, Percent Year-on-Year Change[4]

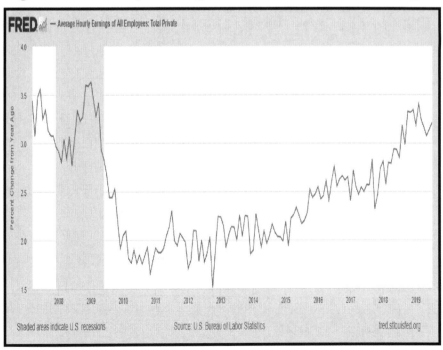

So, those are the three biggest numbers for financial markets in the jobs report — number of jobs created, the unemployment rate, and wage inflation.

In Figure 20-4, you can see the year-on-year percent changes in wage inflation.

For your personal job prospects, I would encourage you to look at the breakdown of job creation and losses in the latest jobs report. The number of jobs lost and created in recent months are shown by sector — like retail, manufacturing, and professional and business services.

As you can tell, there are a lot of important numbers in the jobs report. It's why it is so critical for economists, financial professionals, policy makers, job seekers, and executives.

CHAPTER 21

WEEKLY JOBLESS CLAIMS

Want to know the first sign of a slowing U.S. job market?

It's when people lose their jobs and apply to get paid unemployment benefits.

One of the biggest downsides of a slowing economy is the number of people who lose their jobs, which is why financial analysts, investors, and the mainstream media pay a lot of attention to weekly jobless claims.

Plus, the weekly claims data lead the most critical economic report of the month: the employment report.

The unemployment insurance weekly claims report from the U.S. Department of Labor is called in shorthand "the jobless claims report" by economists and the media. It shows how many people are claiming unemployment insurance after losing their jobs.

This report is usually released on Thursdays, and it shows two important groups of people who are claiming unemployment:

1.) New weekly claims for job losses, which are called *initial claims*. These are people who just became unemployed.

2.) Ongoing weekly claims for unemployed, which are called *continuing claims*. These are people who remained unemployed.

People pay close attention to these numbers for their implications about the job market for a few different reasons.

The initial claims data show how many new people have lost their jobs. Sharp increases in initial claims can happen — and usually do — when the economy slows.

But since most people are unemployed for a period of time after they lose their jobs, a sharp drop in the weekly initial claims is unlikely. After all, people who lose their jobs are still likely to be unemployed for at least a week.

The trend of jobless claims is important because it can show a trend in developments. This can be seen in continuing claims.

After all, continuing claims represent people who have been unemployed for more than a week. They filed for unemployment after their initial filing — not for the first time as with initial claims.

A long-term rise in continuing claims is bad, because it means more people are having trouble finding jobs over a longer term.

Conversely, a long-term decline in continuing claims is good, because it means more people are getting off of unemployment and they are finding jobs.

One of the big things to know about the claims data is that while initial claims can spike fast and show a rapid worsening of the labor market, improvements in continuing claims often take a long time to show up in the data.

The reason: Employers often fire quickly and hire slowly.

Because weekly jobless claims data can shift quickly, it is often a critical signal for the health of the overall U.S. economy.

This means that a trend in good weekly reports can support financial markets over time, but a sharp worsening in jobless claims can cause financial markets — and your investments — to lose value rapidly.

CHAPTER 22

OTHER IMPORTANT EMPLOYMENT DATA

The monthly employment situation report and weekly jobless claims reports are at the top of the list when it comes to critical jobs data. But there are other important related jobs data as well.

There is the Challenger Job Cuts Report, which is produced monthly by the executive outsourcing firm Challenger, Gray & Christmas. This series is based on a compilation of public announcements of layoffs and cuts to jobs reported by companies. It can offer insight into a future net slowdown in the number of jobs created monthly.

Another useful series is the ISM Non-Manufacturing Employment Index. This is a subindex of the ISM Non-Manufacturing Index report and like other ISM series, it has a breakeven of 50. And this series for service sector job creation leads non-farm payrolls.

Finally, there is also the Help Wanted Online series (HWOL). This series shows an index of how many jobs are posted online in a given month. It is produced by The Conference Board and correlated with employment.

Other Critical Economic Data

CHAPTER 23

RETAIL SALES

In the United States, retail sales — the stuff people buy from stores and online — are very important because the U.S. economy is driven largely by the consumption of its population.

Some economies, like China, are more focused on manufacturing, while others, like Saudi Arabia or Nigeria, have commodity-centric economies.

But in the United States, it's our consumption that defines our economy. And the most important monthly report about that consumption is the monthly U.S. Advanced Retail Sales Report.

When Bloomberg or *The Wall Street Journal* write about it, they just call it "retail sales."

Economists and analysts use this report to analyze market trends and determine the direction of the economy. Businesses use this report to measure how they are performing and predict future demand for their products.

Each monthly U.S. retail sales report includes:

- Motor vehicle and parts sales
- Gasoline station sales
- Food and beverage store sales
- Furniture, electronics, and all kinds of other stuff

The two big numbers quoted in the press are the monthly percent change in total monthly retail sales, as well as the monthly sales that exclude motor vehicle and parts sales, which is usually shorthanded as "Retail Sales ex-Autos."

When these numbers go up on a monthly basis, that's a good thing. But it's important to know two things about the retail sales report:

First, during downturns total retail sales rates are very low or negative, but they don't usually remain low or negative for long.

After all, it's very difficult for year-over-year growth rates of retail sales to be negative. That's because the retail sales report does not account for inflation. It reflects what economists call nominal prices.

Since prices tend to rise over time in the economy because of inflation, retail sales data have a natural propensity to rise and remain positive. This means that even when overall economic growth is slower or in recession, the rate of increase in the *value* of total retail sales could rise, because *prices* of the things people buy rise over time anyway.

You can see this trend of persistently positive total retail sales in Figure 23-1. The persistently positive year-on-year rates of growth in retail sales can be seen in Figure 23-2.

The second thing to know is that the advance retail sales report is not an actual reporting of data from all retailers.

The report is based on *estimates* of retail sales using a survey sample of about 5,000 companies, with 1,300 of those being used consistently because of their relatively large effect on the sales of certain industry groups.

Again: It's not an actual number but an estimate.

Figure 23-1: U.S. Total Retail Sales[1]

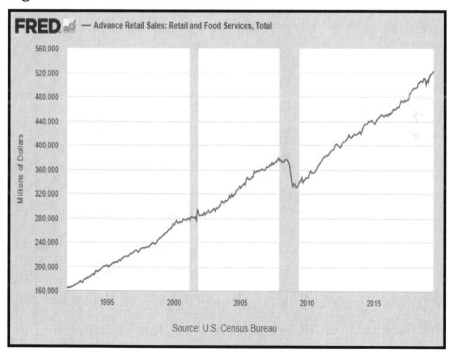

E-Commerce

One of the most important developments for retail sales in recent years has been the rise in e-commerce. This is the value of goods you order online.

In Q4 1999, when it was first measured, e-commerce was only 0.6 percent of total retail sales. But since then, it has risen significantly in both dollar terms — and as a percent of total retail sales. You can see the rise in the value of e-commerce sales in Figure 23-3.

Additionally, in Figure 23-4, you can see the increase of e-commerce as a percent of retail sales.

Figure 23-2: Year-on-Year Growth Rates of Retail Sales[2]

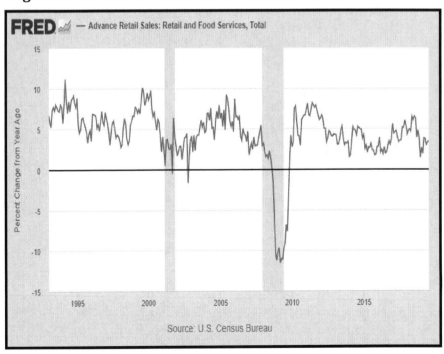

Figure 23-3: Value of U.S. E-Commerce Retail Sales[3]

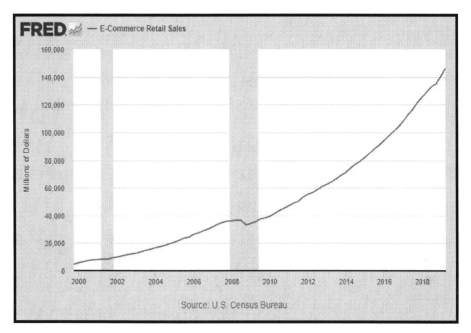

Figure 23-4: E-Commerce as a Percent of Total Retail Sales[4]

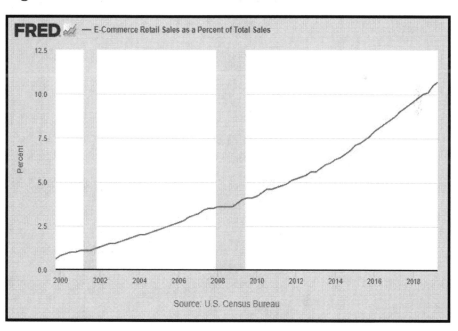

E-commerce is experiencing massive growth, and it is a growing part of the supply chain that operates in the background. It is being driven by fundamental consumer demand, which is nothing short of an unstoppable force, especially in the United States, where consumption is almost 70 percent of the U.S. economy.

And even though Figure 23-4 reflects e-commerce sales in the first quarter of 2019 accounted for 10.2 percent of total sales, this figure is relatively low.

But e-commerce has risen in absolute terms and as a percent of total retail sales. And it's likely to rise a lot more — both in the United States and globally, as is reflected in Figure 23-5.

Figure 23-5: E-Commerce Share of Total Global Retail Sales[5]

If you want to know how the U.S. economy is doing, it's important to watch retail sales. After all, consumption is 70 percent of the U.S. economy.

This is why if retail sales are strong, it's good for growth. But if they slow or fall, this is usually a very bad sign for the economy.

While retail sales data is important for the U.S. economy, it is also absolutely critical for the stock prices of retail companies like Walmart, Target, and Amazon. And it is important the stock market overall.

CHAPTER 24

VEHICLE SALES

One of the most expensive purchases you can make is to buy a vehicle.

This is why there are a lot of advertisements for cars on TV, on the radio, in the paper, and online. Companies want you to buy their new cars.

New car purchases are good for the economy, too, because new car sales become part of U.S. gross domestic product — or GDP.

Unfortunately, used car sales don't contribute to GDP. But because new sales contribute to U.S. economic growth, new vehicle sales are important for economic data.

This sales data is called "Light Weight Vehicle Sales." This report includes monthly sales for cars and light trucks, which also includes SUVs.

The number of vehicles sold is released at the very beginning of the next month. In other words, cars sold in June will be released at the very beginning of July.

And the number of cars sold is not quoted in dollars, nor is it the actual number of cars sold. Instead, the vehicle sales number is a seasonally adjusted annual rate, or SAAR. You can see this below in Figure 24-1.

That means that the number you see in the press, which may be 17, 18, or 19 million, represents the expected number of cars that would be sold during an entire year based on the current month's sales.

Figure 24-1: U.S. Light Vehicle Sales[1]

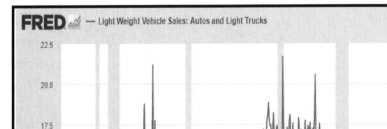

But the SAAR isn't quite the actual level of monthly sales multiplied by 12, because it includes adjustments for seasonal dynamics — like a potential drop-off during the winter due to cold weather or high sales in months with holidays like Memorial Day and Labor Day. Believe it or not, those kinds of sales are accounted for in the seasonal adjustments, because they have historically impacted sales data in given months in a way that would otherwise overstate the annualized likely rate of vehicles sales.

Additionally, it is important to note that the media-cited vehicle sales SAAR figure does not include heavy-weight trucks, although there are data released monthly for heavy-weight trucks.

Figure 24-2: U.S. Heavy-Weight Trucks[2]

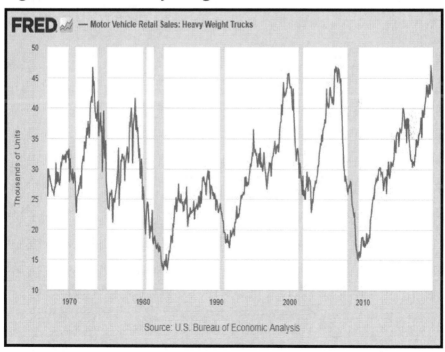

Implications

So what do vehicle sales mean for the economy?

During years of positive economic growth, vehicle sales are usually strong. In fact, without strong vehicle sales, it's tough to have a strong economy.

This means that the number of vehicles sold is important for related investments — like the stock and bond prices of Ford, GM, and Toyota. And because vehicle sales are critical for the broader economy, these sales numbers can impact the entire stock market and even the bond market.

And the heavy-weight truck sales is even more important for the overall economy, because it serves as a proxy for business activity, CapEx, and overall U.S. commerce.

There are also other related monthly vehicle data that are important for gauging the health of the overall U.S. economy. The data released monthly by the Bureau of Economic Analysis include data about vehicle inventories and exports along with data released identifying vehicles as domestically produced units as well as units produced in Canada and Mexico.

Another data series related to vehicle sales that is also a proxy for growth is miles driven. While this series includes total miles driven for all vehicles, it is an important proxy for overall economic activity. And, of course, with ever greater miles driven comes greater needs to maintain, repair, and — most importantly — replace vehicles.

You can see the long-term trend in rising miles driven in Figure 24-3.

Gasoline

Heavy-weight trucks generally use diesel fuel, but when people talk about U.S. light vehicle sales, they also talk about gasoline.

And while fuel prices impact vehicle sales, they do not impact the number of vehicles sold.

But they often impact the types of vehicles that are sold. That makes sense because the total cost of ownership of an SUV or light truck is higher than for a car, when you consider fuel costs.

Figure 24-3: U.S. Total Miles Driven[3]

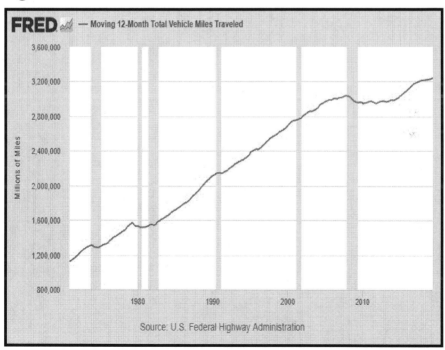

In fact, between 2005 and 2015, when gasoline prices went up, SUV and light truck sales went down as a percent of total light vehicles sold.

This inverse correlation held for about a decade, although it has recently broken down due to persistently low gasoline prices. You can see this dynamic in Figure 24-4.

This means that for a decade, people's decisions about what kind of vehicle to purchase — a car or a light truck — was often not based on the price of the car or the health of the economy, but it was based on the price of gasoline the car buyer might have seen at a gas station on the way to the car dealership.

Figure 24-4: Gasoline Prices and Percent Light Truck Sales[4]

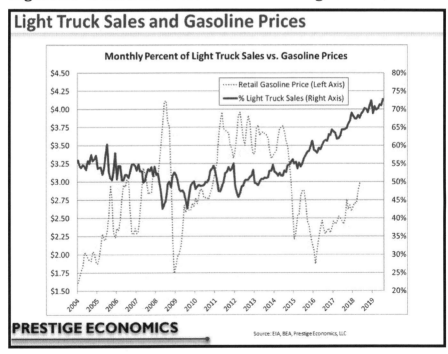

The monthly light vehicle sales data is currently one of the trickier economic data series to find.

It is produced by the U.S. Bureau of Economic Analysis and the report is listed as "Motor Vehicles" under "Supplemental Information and Additional Data" here:

https://www.bea.gov/data/gdp/gross-domestic-product

CHAPTER 25

INDUSTRIAL PRODUCTION

Have you ever had someone call you industrious? It means that you're hard working.

And if you want to know if the U.S. economy is working hard, you should be watching industrial production data, which is a measure of how much manufacturing, mining, and utilities industries are producing in the U.S. economy.

This data is produced by the Federal Reserve, and most analysts and media personalities focus on monthly percent changes.

But the really important part of the industrial production data is the trend in long-term levels of total industrial activity.

Industrial production is measured across a few key product groups, including consumer goods (durables like autos as well as nondurables like clothing), business equipment (like machinery and IT equipment), construction, and materials (textiles, paper, chemicals, and energy).

Because the U.S. economy usually grows and expands, industrial production is almost always growing year over year, as you can see in Figure 25-1.

In fact, if we look at data back through 1919, you can see that so far industrial production has only contracted year over year during recessions with one exception: It contracted year over year during 2015 and 2016, when there was no recession.

This coincident indictor reflects what one would expect: It expands during years of growth and contracts around times of economic contractions.

Figure 25-1: Industrial Production[1]

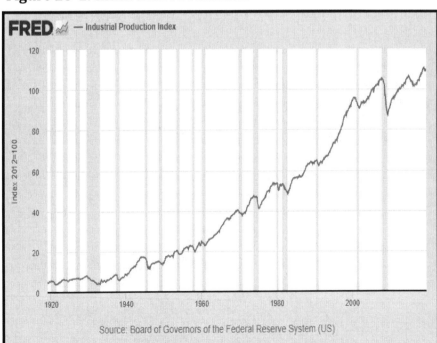

This relationship between industrial production growth and GDP growth can be seen in Figure 25-2.

Capacity Utilization

The industrial production report also includes other data that often gets overlooked: something known as capacity utilization which some call CAPU.

Like industrial production, capacity utilization demonstrates cyclical dynamics, whereby it usually falls during recessions and rebounds during economic recoveries.

Figure 25-2: Industrial Production Year-on-Year Growth[2]

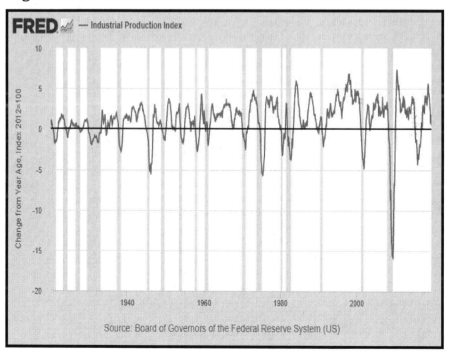

Source: Board of Governors of the Federal Reserve System (US)

Capacity utilization is important because is shows how much slack there is in certain parts of the economy. It also has a limit of 100 percent.

This is different than industrial production, which has no limit, because industrial production shows how much is being produced, rather than the percent utilization of the capacity in place. A high level of capacity utilization is positive for manufacturing and industrial companies.

And capacity utilization is usually at its best during the peak of a business cycle — and at its lowest during recessions, as you can see in Figure 25-3.

Figure 25-3: Capacity Utilization[3]

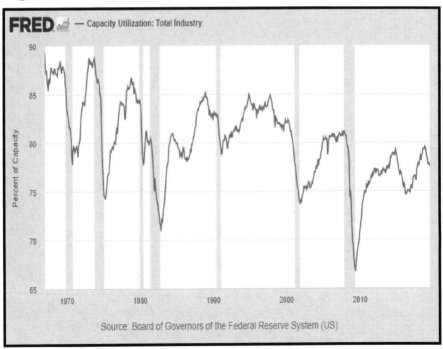

Source: Board of Governors of the Federal Reserve System (US)

While industrial production is pretty straightforward, capacity utilization can be a more difficult concept. So, let me give you an example of capacity utilization.

Let's say there is a factory that manufactures cars. The factory can manufacture 100 cars a day, but it only manufactures 90. The capacity is 100. The utilization of that capacity is 90 out of 100 — or 90 percent.

If that auto company is running at 99 percent utilization, that means it is really cranking out cars. That's probably good for its stock price, and it's good for its workers — and planned hiring.

But if the utilization rate is only 60 percent, that's bad.

If utilization is low or goes down, companies in those industries could see their profitability fall, because they don't have enough orders to fill.

This means they have slack in their businesses; they may need to lay off people. And their stock prices could fall.

Most companies measure their production levels. But does your company or industry measure its capacity utilization?

If utilization is high, your company is probably doing well — and it might need to expand, grow, and hire more people. But if the utilization is low, you may wish to start looking around for other professional opportunities.

Housing Data

CHAPTER 26

HOUSING OVERVIEW

When housing was rocking in the mid-2000s, I bought my first home. It was a condo. One day, I came home from work, and a lady in a car was sitting in the parking lot of my building. And she shouted out to me, "Hey, do you live here?"

I told her I did, and then she asked me how long I'd lived there. It had been about a year. And she wanted to know how much my home price had risen.

I told her I had no idea. It was true.

She was shocked. She asked me, "How could you not know what your home is worth?"

I told her I bought it because the monthly payment was low. She thought I was crazy. I had actually bought a home to live in it, and I was only concerned with the monthly affordability of my mortgage payment, which included both principal and interest.

Even though I only thought of my home in terms of its affordability on a monthly basis, most people care a lot about the value of their home, because it is their biggest asset.

For many people, a mortgage is a way to get a tax deduction, and it's a way to force themselves to save money, by building up equity — or ownership — in a piece of property.

Since a home is most people's biggest investment, it's a major concern to most people: Everyone has to buy or rent a place to live; talking about the housing market is also a pretty standard conversation among professionals and friends, and at parties.

Fortunately, there are a lot of housing reports with data to help you gain perspective on the sector. It will help you understand and talk about housing in these settings, but I wouldn't count on a strong grasp of home sales and price data to make you the life of the party.

But it's a start...right?

Do you know what they call an economist with a sense of humor...? It's an accountant. And now you know why.

Anyone who owns a house or is thinking of buying a house cares about home prices — or at least the monthly mortgage payments they would be making to own a house, compared to renting.

Logically, home prices are impacted — like all markets — by supply and demand.

But since this is a real-world market, home prices are also impacted by the potential future supply of new homes available, potential future demand (which can be influenced by interest rates), as well as recent average and median prices of homes sold.

All of this data is spread across a lot of economic reports, and being familiar with them before buying a house — or making a rent-versus-buy decision — could be valuable.

The most important housing data reports include:
- New Homes Sales
- Existing Home Sales
- Pending Home Sales
- MBA Mortgage Applications
- Housing Starts and Building Permits
- S&P Case Shiller Index

Home sales are also impacted by the level of interest rates, so looking at interest rates can be important for determining future mortgage rates — and how adjustable rate mortgages will change. Higher interest rates tend to cause housing activity to slow, while lower interest rates support housing.

Housing data can do a *lot* for you! It can give you perspective on where home sales are, what pricing looks like, and what activity is in the pipeline. These kinds of data are important if you want to know what your house might be worth — of if you are thinking about buying or selling a home.

Housing data can also be important when considering investing in real estate — or investing in a company exposed to real estate activity, like a construction company, lumber company, door manufacturer, or appliance company.

Finally, housing data can be important if you are considering a profession in real estate as well.

In this section of *Reading the Economic Tea Leaves*, we will look more deeply at some of the most important indicators of housing activity, as well as some of the key drivers of sales and prices.

For a full list of housing indicators and where to find them, check out the Data Appendix at the back of this book.

CHAPTER 27

HOUSING STARTS

People talk about building their dream home. But a dream home is just a dream — until the work crew shows up and starts digging the foundation, pouring the concrete, and putting up the house frame.

Once that happens, it is a dream housing start.

Everyone wants to know what's going to happen to home sales, from politicians and government economists (because it's important for growth), investors in GE and Whirlpool (because it's important for appliance sales), and commodity traders (because you need lumber and copper to build a house).

So, how can we forecast the number of new homes that will be sold? What data would be most helpful? It's probably the number of new houses that have already started construction.

After all, you can't sell a house you haven't started building.

Housing starts represents the number of homes that have seen construction start in a certain month. Each housing start in September represents a new home that started to be built in September.

And what we mean here by starting a house is when the construction on a new home actually begins and breaks ground. This is the most important leading economic indicator of homes sold.

So if you decide to build your own dream house, the day the construction crew shows up and starts building is the day your house will be counted as started.

Housing starts are based on surveys of home builders, and they are part of a monthly report produced by the U.S. Census Bureau and the U.S. Department of Housing and Urban Development.

So what kind of housing starts data can you expect to see every month?

Starts data includes seasonally adjusted annual rates otherwise known as the SAAR.

So, if you see a number for housing starts like 1200K (this is how it is quoted), it means 1.2 million new housing starts per year — *if* the current month is representative for activity in the whole year. And that 1200K or 1.2 million is the number you see on CNBC, quoted in *The Wall Street Journal*, or discussed on Bloomberg Radio.

There are also non-seasonally adjusted rates and historical actual data. And the report also shows data for different kinds of housing.

After all, not all homes are for one family, or what finance people call "single-family homes."

Right?

A dream *house* probably only has one unit, but a dream duplex would have two units, and a dream condo complex might have four, five, or more units.

And we'd still need to count those starts. And those data are broken down in reports.

But each kind of structure single family or multiunit counts as just *one* start.

These so-called multiunit starts are even more important for appliance makers like Maytag and Kenmore, because each unit is likely to require a refrigerator, washer, dryer, and other appliances.

There is an important regional breakdown in the report that can offer hints about coming regional construction job needs, regional appliance sales, home sales, and real estate opportunities. And this data is shown in four different geographical areas: Northeast, Midwest, West, and South.

Big companies in one of these areas in one of these fields can expect their share prices to move on this data. Home Depot might decide where to put its next stores based on where construction is taking place. So might Target or Walmart.

Plus, stockbrokers may decide to sell stock in homebuilders depending on housing starts data. After all, if fewer homes are started, fewer homes will be sold in the future.

Politicians, central bankers, and government economists also watch housing starts for their economic implications.

After all, more homes equals more growth.

A main contributing factor of the Great Recession from 2007 to 2009 in the United States was the burst in the housing bubble.

Because the housing market burst, housing credit was tight for years, which was why U.S. growth after 2009 was sluggish.

Mortgages became tough to get, fewer homes could be bought, and fewer homes were started. But this kind of dynamic has happened before. Housing starts often weaken during economic downturns and then they rise during periods of monetary stimulus and economic recovery.

In this manner, you can see that housing starts can be an important leading indicator for an entire economy.

But that isn't always the case. And it certainly wasn't in the wake of the Great Recession. In fact, the recovery of housing starts following the Great Recession was extremely slow. It's part of the reason why the U.S. economy was sluggish to recover after 2009.

Furthermore, even at its strongest levels since the Great Recession ended in mid-2009, housing starts have remained persistently weak and at levels normally consistent with recessions. You can see this in Figure 27-1.

But whether they rise or fall, housing starts lead home sales. And that means they lead a part of economic growth.

Figure 27-1: Housing Starts[1]

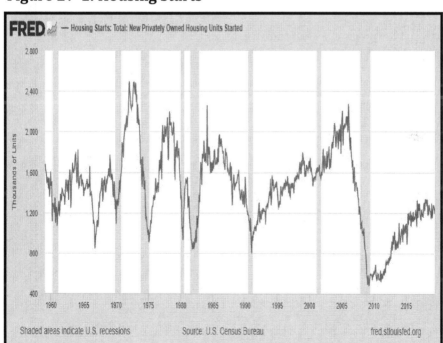

CHAPTER 28

BUILDING PERMITS

People say it's better to beg for forgiveness than ask permission, but I can tell you one area where that isn't true: building a house.

You need permission to build a home.

Even before you start building your dream home, you need to file some paperwork. The process begins with a building permit since this is where the whole party starts; building permits are a key indicator of new home sales and how construction contributes to economic growth.

Building permits are the most upstream economic indicator for housing that exists in the United States. In fact, they give the earliest glimpse into what's likely to happen to housing activity.

Building permits are a measure of privately-owned housing units authorized by building permits.

Because this is for private housing, it's just for homes.

Like housing starts, building permits data include a breakdown of seasonally adjusted annual rates, as well as non-seasonally adjusted monthly and annual historical rates for three categories of home permits:

- 1 unit, which is single-family and the majority of permits
- 2 to 4 units
- and 5 units or more

Also, as with other housing data, the data is broken down into four regions, as shown in Figure 28-1:

- Northeast
- Midwest
- South
- West

Figure 28-1: Building Permits Regions[1]

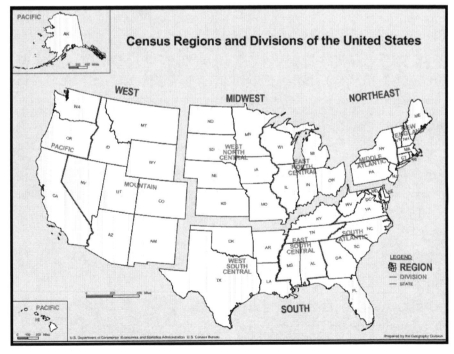

Given the move from the Rust Belt to the Sun Belt in recent years, the most action for new building permits — like housing — has been in the south for years, which is likely to be true for many years to come.

Building permits are released in the same report with housing starts, and permits are usually higher than starts. Of course, not everybody completes what they permit, and not all permitted homes will be started or completed.

This makes building permits a bit more of a speculative leading indicator of new home sales than, say, housing starts.

In the press, permits are quoted as a seasonally adjusted annual rate or SAAR. So the number you'd see quoted in *The Wall Street Journal* or on CNBC might be something like 1300K, or 1.3 million building permits.

But this isn't the number of permits for the month, but it's the rate for the year based on that month's performance, and taking into consideration seasonal factors — like weather.

The Value of Building Permits

Building permits provide the greatest leading indication into coming regional construction job needs, regional appliance sales, home sales, and real estate opportunities.

And building permits data can also have important implications for specific companies.

High levels of permits can indicate that a company like D.R. Horton — the biggest home builder in the country — will be hiring to start building new homes. And it can also indicate that a lumber company like Weyerhaeuser will need to prepare lumber for sale in the region.

This also means that stock prices of homebuilders that operate in regions with rising building permits are likely to see their share prices move on this data.

That makes sense, right? If a company is building houses in the southern region, and data jumps in that region unexpectedly, that company's stock price is likely to go up.

And lumber prices can move on the overall national number. After all, you need wood to build most homes!

The market impact of building permits is strongest when building permits data moves in the same direction as housing starts. If they both go up, or if they both go down, that can be a big deal!

And what drives building permits? Economic growth, jobs, and low interest rates. If the economy is good, people have jobs, and if money is cheap, people will be building new homes — and they will have to file building permits first.

Building permits can lead the business cycle as they did going into the Great Recession, which lasted from the end of 2007 to mid-2009.

But generally, building permits move with the economy and counter to interest rates. This is why cuts in interest rates and economic recoveries have historically sent building permits higher, while increases in interest rates have historically slowed building permits. You can see this dynamic in Figure 28-2.

But because not all permits become housing starts, let alone sales, building permits are a bit more speculative as a data point. As such, building permits are a bit of a gift. You have to accept them, but what you do with them is up to you. After all, permits can both lead growth, and they can also underperform, since not all permitted homes will be built or sold.

Figure 28-2: Building Permits[2]

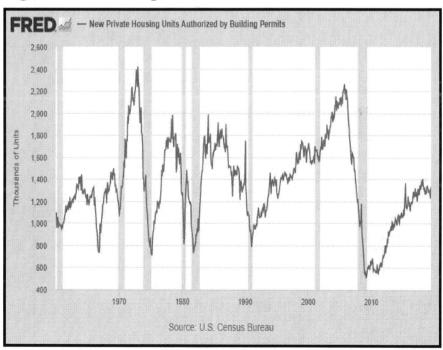

CHAPTER 29

NEW HOME SALES

When the average person asks about the housing market, they're really asking one basic question: "How is the value of my biggest investment doing?"

There are a lot of economic indicators about housing and construction activity, but there are only a few reports that indicate value. And the New Home Sales Report from the U.S. Census Bureau is one of the most important reports that does.

If you want to know what it will cost to buy a new home — and how many new homes are available for sale nationally (and regionally) — this is the report for you.

New home sales data are also important for the overall economy, because new homes are part of GDP growth, and more new homes equals more GDP.

Residential investment averages roughly 3 to 5 percent of GDP, according to the National Association of Home Builders.

This includes construction of new single-family and multifamily structures, residential remodeling, production of manufactured homes, and brokers' fees.

So if new home sales rise, GDP is likely to rise as well, whereas weakness in new home sales is likely to weigh on GDP.

Plus, beyond that 3 to 5 percent, new home sales also lead to new appliance sales, the purchase of new furniture, and other household items. So each new home sale has a big economic impact.

This is why the monthly New Home Sales Report is hotly watched.

The report is released by the U.S. Census Bureau and the U.S. Department of Housing and Urban Development jointly, and it focuses only on single-family home sales; not on condos, townhomes, or other multifamily new homes.

New home sales are quoted in a seasonally adjusted annual rate — or SAAR. So if you see a big number like 700K on CNBC next April, that doesn't mean 700,000 new homes were sold in April. That would be just crazy!

That's the number of homes that would be sold in a year based on the level of the homes solid in April. It's more complicated than multiplying that monthly number by 12, but that's kind of what it's like. The trend in the SAAR can be seen in Figure 29-1.

Of course, the reports also include the actual number of new homes sold every month.

These are called "unadjusted numbers," and they can be misleading, because weather dynamics and other seasonal factors can really impact new home sales in a big way! Things like demand for homes in spring and summer to get kids in new schools before the fall.

The New Home Sales Report also includes "Months' Supply" of new homes available for sale. A lot of new home supply is bad for prices, but tight new home supply supports prices. That economic truth translates in the housing market as well!

Figure 29-1: New Home Sales, SAAR[1]

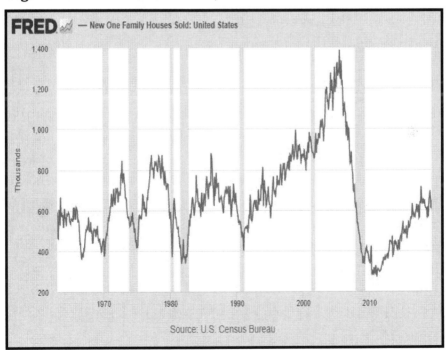

Speaking of prices, the New Home Sales Report also includes the average and median sales prices of new homes sold, as well as price ranges — and a percentage distribution of prices for new home sales. This ends up looking like a bell curve of new home prices; some are high, some are low, but most are in the middle.

It's important to know that even though most people would define inflation as "living in a more expensive house without actually moving," the increases in new home prices aren't captured in inflation.

But home prices are important for people's wealth!

Of course, home prices are sensitive to interest rates. After all, most homes are not paid for with cash. They are financed with mortgages. When interest rates are higher, you have to allocate more of your monthly payment to the interest rate of the mortgage, and you can afford less house.

When my parents bought their first house in the late 1970s, the sticker price was cheap around $52,000, but the interest rate was crazy at 12 percent.

In comparison, when I bought my house in 2013, the interest rate was under 4 percent, but the sticker price for the house was many multiples of my parents' home price — for a similarly sized house.

As you can see, there are tradeoffs between mortgage rates and home prices!

For new and existing home buyers, it's generally true that lower interest rates can send home prices higher (since people can buy "more house"), while higher interest rates can send home prices lower (since people are forced to buy "less house")

New home sale prices are reported as both median and average prices at the national level and in the four census regions. The national median price can be seen in Figure 29-2.

The most distinctive thing about this data is the massive drop seen after the Great Recession and the rise thereafter, especially following the third round of the Federal Reserve's quantitative easing program and central bank balance sheet expansion.

Figure 29-2: New Home Sales, Median Prices[2]

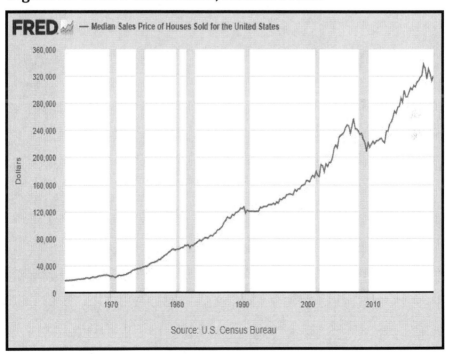

On an individual level, the new home sales report can have value as well. After all, if you want to buy a new house, browse before you buy — and take a look at the New Home Sales Report.

Look at the average and median prices — and where there are homes for sale regionally as well as the number of homes in inventory.

CHAPTER 30

EXISTING HOME SALES

Ever wondered why people don't call existing homes used homes or vintage homes, but they talk about vintage clothes and used cars?

The words may be different, but vintage clothes, used cars, and existing homes all do have one thing in common: They don't contribute positively to GDP.

Only new stuff counts.

But the number of existing homes sold — which are quoted in the millions — far exceeds the level of new home sales in the United States, which is quoted in the thousands.

This means that while new home sales are important for GDP, the best gauge of the value of your home — of the price of your home — is really the data that comes out of monthly existing home sales report. And there's even data about regional prices in that report.

Every month, the National Association of Realtors (NAR) releases data on the number of existing homes sold, the inventory of homes available for sale, and the prices of homes sold — by region.

You can find the monthly report on the NAR website here: **https://www.nar.realtor/research-and-statistics/housing-statistics/existing-home-sales**

The existing home sales report also includes an inventory figure. This represents the number of homes available for sale divided by the current level of sales.

So if the current level of actual monthly sales is 400,000 homes and the number of homes available for sale is 2 million, then the number of months of inventory would be five.

You take the 2 million divide it by the 400,000 homes sold in the current month and that's where the five comes from.

If no additional existing homes go up for sale in the next five months, the river will run dry and there won't be any more existing homes that could be sold. Inventory would be zero.

Of course, this isn't going to happen, but when that inventory number is low, it indicates the housing market is tight — and it can send home prices up.

Prices

Existing home prices are influenced by a few key factors.

First, recent prices of existing homes impact the current prices. This is why people care about how much their neighbor's house sells for.

Because it influences the price you can get. This data is reported in the existing home sales report on a national and regional level.

Second, there's the existing homes in inventory we just discussed.

How many homes are on the market?

If it's a lot, that hurts prices. But a tight market keeps prices up.

Finally, home prices are sensitive to interest rates, because most people don't pay cash for their homes. This is the same dynamic that impacts what people can pay for new homes as well.

Lower interest rates can send existing home prices higher (since people can buy "more house"), while higher interest rates can send existing home prices lower (since people are forced to buy "less house").

Rising existing home prices can make homeowners wealthier — and it can provide homeowners the opportunity to access equity credit lines, which happened in the mid-2000's when countless analysts on CNBC often said that people "used their homes as ATM machines."

The subsequent spending can bolster economic growth. But the actual sale of existing homes does not count toward GDP the way new home sales do.

Existing home sales data also have a different timing component than new home sales.

Because new home sales happen when a new home is bought. If it's bought in January. It's in the January new homes sales report.

But existing home sales have to "close" in a complicated paperwork pile up required to transfer ownership of a property.

And it can take 30 days, 45 days, or even more than 60 days to line up all the paperwork for a home to close.

This means that the existing home sales report for January that reflects January closes might include homes that went to contract in January, December — and as far back as November or even earlier. It just depends on how the closes were scheduled.

Do you know anyone who has bought a house?

Ask them how long it took to close on their property. Chances are, it took more than a month. And they will probably describe the process as a crazy sprint.

This is why existing home sales lag new home sales.

CHAPTER 31

PENDING HOME SALES

No one likes to wait for things. And one of the most annoying things you will wait for in life is likely to be the close on a home.

It's nutty. You have to organize and check paperwork, firm up your financing, and do a ton of other little things.

And it's unpleasant for both the buyer and the seller. Everyone is often running around to get everything squared away at the last minute.

Plus, whether you are selling an existing home and can't wait to cash out, or you are buying an existing home and can't wait to move in, you still will likely have to wait 30 days, 45 days, or even longer to be able to actually execute the contract in a process called "closing."

This process also makes home sales data messy. New home sales are recorded when the home is bought, but existing home sales are only recorded after the "closing," even if the agreement was made months in advance.

To solve the messy data issue and offer more transparency into existing home sales activity, the National Association of Realtors (NAR) created an economic indicator to show the level of pending home sales.

This provides clarity on the actual level of sales activity, which can impact home prices — and the prospect of selling a house.

Every month, the NAR releases a Pending Home Sales Index that is designed to be a leading indicator of existing home sales activity.

This index measures housing contract activity for signed agreements of existing single-family homes, condos, and co-ops. If it's residential, it's included!

The pending home sales data reflects that nail-biting period, when buyers and sellers are just hoping the deal gets done and the contract is signed.

And a lot of things can be in those contracts. When I bought my house, I included in the contract that I wanted the two pink flamingos in the lawn to be included in the deal.

I got my flamingos — and the house. But I had to wait for the close.

Pending Home Sales Index is Different
The pending home sales report is very different than other housing data.

First, it is an index — not an annualized number of contracts.

And there's no information on prices or inventories.

Since it is an index without prices, the highest value for the pending home sales data is in its trend over time for gauging activity. If the pending home sales index falls hard, then existing home sales will fall too.

You can't sell a house without a contract in the works.

And a drop in sales weighs on home prices.

You can find this report at the NAR website here:
https://www.nar.realtor/research-and-statistics/housing-statistics/pending-home-sales

What has the trend been for pending home sales? If it's going up, this is supportive for home prices.

But if it's falling, this could weigh on prices.

As an individual, this could impact your decision about buying, selling, or listing a home.

CHAPTER 32

MBA MORTGAGE APPLICATIONS

Being familiar with mortgage data provides insight into the pace of home sales — and the levels of different mortgage rates.

Knowledge is power, and knowing the cost of mortgage rates before applying can give you valuable leverage — and save you tens of thousands of dollars — and it might keep you from overpaying.

I once had a professor who said that a mortgage puts you in the same position as a medieval serf, with a stone around his neck. And yet, that's how most homes are financed, because most people don't have the cash to buy a house outright.

Mortgages show us that there are two sides to every market: a side selling and a side buying. When looking at U.S. housing, some analysts focus on permits that need to be filed, homes that need to be started, and homes that become pending sales after they go under contract. That is all on the side of the market that is selling homes.

But before a home is sold and before it comes under contract, there needs to be a buyer.

And since most people don't pay cash outright for their homes, the buyer needs to apply for a mortgage. This is why mortgage applications are a key leading indicator of home sales — and important for the overall economy.

The Mortgage Bankers Association (MBA) releases a Weekly Mortgage Applications Survey using a series of indexed activity. The shorthand for this index is MBA Mortgage Applications.

One thing that can be confusing about this indicator is the name: MBA Mortgage Applications. This isn't the number of people who have an MBA — a Master's of Business Administration — who are applying for or issuing mortgages. This is a data point compiled by the industry group for mortgage bankers — the Mortgage Bankers Association. That's the MBA here.

This indicator is important, because if people aren't applying for mortgages, they aren't planning on buying homes. But if people are applying, they will be buying more homes.

This indicator is quoted as a week-over-week percentage change in mortgage activity. And while this report is released every week, it is particularly important over longer periods of time. If it falls week after week after week, there is a compounding effect of a worsening trend. If it rises week after week, there is a compounding effect of an improving trend.

The data covers over 75 percent of all U.S. retail residential mortgage applications, so it should give you a pretty good idea as to the activity and rates for mortgages.

But there isn't just one type of mortgage. And the weekly MBA data includes a breakdown of some of the main categories of mortgage activities.

This includes new mortgages for home purchases — like when I bought a house in 2013. I got a 30-year mortgage at 4 percent.

There are also refinance mortgages — this usually happens when interest rates fall. I refinanced in 2015 because the interest rate had fallen from 4 percent to 3 percent. There is usually a cost to refinance your mortgage, and a 1 percentage point difference was worth it for me!

Plus, there are also adjustable rate mortgages — otherwise known as ARMs. The rates of these mortgages change over the life of the mortgage — and they are quite complicated.

These were also one of the sources of trouble leading up to the financial crisis of 2007 to 2009.

There's even a breakdown of average interest rates by mortgage type. So, no matter what kind of mortgage you are interested in, there are likely average current rates in the MBA report.

CHAPTER 33

CONSTRUCTION SPENDING

Have you ever heard the 1980s song "We Built This City on Rock and Roll"?

Well, if construction spending were tied to rock and roll, it might not be as important an economic indicator.

But as it turns out, construction spending is very important for U.S. economic growth.

Plus, construction spending is important for building materials and can impact the demand and prices of copper (for wire and plumbing), plastic pipe (for plumbing), steel for bigger structures, and lumber for single-family homes, condos, and townhouses.

Because construction spending is critical for overall economic growth — and a number of commodity markets — it is an important data point for specific companies, some industries, and *big* economic policy stuff.

Economists, investors, and traders are very interested in construction sales. And the number they are hungry for is the month-on-month percent change in the value of construction put in place. This includes all kinds of things that are "put in place" in each month.

Everything from new toilets to lumber to project management and design of the project are included. As well as architectural and engineering costs, overhead, interest and taxes, and contractor's profits.

This is part of the Monthly Construction Spending Report from the U.S. Census Bureau. And you can find it online here: **https://www.census.gov/construction/c30/c30index.html**

The monthly report also segments out these expenses into different categories of *private* residential and non-residential construction as well as *public* residential and non-residential construction. And some of the categories get very detailed!
— Gyms: These are listed in the report as private, non-residential, amusement and recreation, fitness construction.
— Rest Stops: These are listed as public, non-residential, state and local, transportation, rest stop construction.

Those are in there too! And more!

There are annualized breakouts of construction expenses for all kinds of industries. So if you wanted to determine how manufacturing, lodging, malls, or drugstores are doing, this could be an important report.

Plus, new facilities also need more people to work at them. This means if you "follow the money" for construction, it could also show you what sectors will — or will not be hiring.

If you do research on industries or work in consulting, you need to be able to identify the activity and prospects for specific economic sectors like commercial real estate, education, or power generation. This is why the Construction Spending Report can be very helpful, because it shows you levels of activity and investment in construction for those industries. There are also broad-based economic implications for the trend in construction overall. And this can impact government spending and interest rates.

While government construction spending tends to remain unchanged in a slow economy (or even rise), private construction spending tends to rise when interest rates fall and slow when interest rates go up. As with most big expenditures — and most real estate — there is an inverse relationship between construction and interest rates.

Interest rates were a lot higher in the 1980s than they are today. Maybe that's why they had to build that city on rock and roll. Interest rates were probably just too high to finance all the steel cement, wood, and copper.

If you have investments in a sector like power generation, commercial real estate, or health care, looking at the construction activity in those sectors could provide insights into the health of those investments.

GDP Growth Data

CHAPTER 34

GDP OVERVIEW

Wouldn't it be nice if there was one common way to talk about economic growth? Fortunately, there is!

When people talk broadly about the actual rate of growth in an economy, they are almost always talking about GDP, which stands for gross domestic product.

When people say the U.S. economy grew at 2 percent last year or Germany grew by 3 percent last quarter, they are talking about GDP. And GDP includes all new activity — all new goods and services — produced inside the borders of a country.

GDP is comprised of four main categories of growth activity:
- **Consumption** — what people are buying.
- **Business Investment** — what companies are spending their money on to grow.
- **Net Exports** — the balance of trade (exports minus imports), which can be negative.
- **Government Spending** — what the government is spending money on.

It's important to know that these four components are part of GDP in any economy.

GDP includes everything new that is made in an economy: all the new cars, new construction, new schools, new investments, and new government expenditures.

In the United States, the Bureau of Economic Analysis — or BEA — is tasked with pulling together all of the growth data in the economy. And these reports are released quarterly.

The most important number to watch in the GDP report is the percent change for the quarter-over-quarter annualized real GDP growth rate.

That sounds like a mouthful, and it is. But it is the rate of GDP growth quoted in the press.

They usually just say, "GDP rose by 3.1 percent in Q1" or "GDP fell by 1.5 percent."

They leave out all the sticky details that get you to an annualized rate of change, based on the level of GDP compared to the previous quarter.

Two other things about this quarter-over-quarter growth rate quoted in the press: This is also a seasonally adjusted growth rate to strip out seasonal factors like holiday retail sales or summer vacations, and it is "real" because it strips out inflation.

You see, economic growth can be measured in current prices, or it can account for inflation.

Real GDP excludes inflation, showing real growth. And this is the number people want to know: They want to know how the economy is growing without including inflation. Because prices usually rise, and that can be deceiving.

Of course, there is a way to measure GDP plus inflation. And that's called nominal GDP. That shows growth in current dollar values.

If the economy grows by 5 percent and that includes 2 percent inflation, nominal GDP is all of that: It's 5 percent. But real GDP excludes inflation, which is 3 percent — the 5 percent nominal GDP minus the 2 percent inflation.

You will almost never see nominal GDP quoted in the press.

When it comes to GDP, the press is trying to "keep it real."

While GDP is an important economic indicator, there are a couple of big drawbacks to the U.S. GDP reports.

This report is only released quarterly in the United States and in most economies. This means that it isn't the most up-to-date data series, which is why other economic reports that are more timely are so important. Plus, this report is revised a lot. So whatever the growth rate is reported to be, you can expect it will change. That makes planning and policy decisions more difficult.

The report for a given quarter is actually released three times, with the third report released almost three months after the end of the quarter that the GDP report is about.

So a report for the first quarter (January through March) will be released in its advance form at the end of April, preliminary at the end of May, and final at the end of June.

This means that the year is almost half over before you know what growth in January looked like.

Yikes!

Plus, the final number is still highly likely to be revised again in future multiyear revisions!

Just to recap: This super important report about U.S. growth is both highly revised and kind of old (in economic terms) by the time you actually know what's going on. This is why we need all the other economic data that is more timely.

Do you know how much GDP grew last year? What about last quarter? You can find all of this information on www.bea.gov. And I will discuss the most important parts and attributes of GDP in the following chapters of this section.

CHAPTER 35

GDP VERSUS GNP

We live in a global economy, but whether we are talking about England, Mexico, or Russia, economists measure growth for every country in the world by using the same metric: GDP, otherwise known as gross domestic product.

But it's also important to be able to compare what growth looks like across different economies in our global economy.

Today, GDP is the measure people use when talking about growth.

But not long ago, people used something called GNP — gross national product — to talk about growth. Some people still use it today. And it's important to know the difference and why GDP is the better measure of growth.

You see, GNP referred to growth in businesses with a certain national origin, even if they were in foreign countries, but it excluded foreign companies operating in that country.

So Toyotas made in the USA would not be a part of U.S. GNP, but Fords made in Europe would be part of U.S. GNP.

For GDP, Toyotas made in the USA are a part of U.S. GDP. They are not a part of Japanese GDP. Conversely, Fords made in Europe are part of European GDP, not U.S. GDP.

But you want to know about growth where you live — you care about where the job opportunities are and less about the reconciliation of global corporate profits.

So you shouldn't care who owns the companies.

And workers, policymakers, and analysts all feel the same way.

In the United States, the GDP report is produced by the Bureau of Economic Analysis, and that report includes a few lines of data for GNP.

But GNP data are listed as "addenda" — these are sort of "add-ons" in the report.

GNP is essentially an afterthought.

And, of course, it's no longer quoted in the press or watched by finance people.

But occasionally, you will come across a professional or academic talking about GNP. Anyone talking about GNP is just not "in the know."

As a reference point, you can see U.S. GDP versus U.S. GNP in Figure 35-1.

In general, however, GNP could be massive, but no one would even notice — or care. It's just no longer a thing.

Simply put: It's not a number that moves financial markets.

So don't get caught up in the hype if you come across someone talking about GNP, and be sure to wipe GNP from your vocabulary. GDP is the number to watch and talk about — no matter what country you're in!

Figure 35-1: GDP Versus GNP[1]

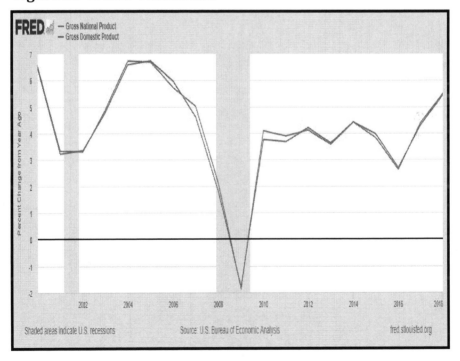

CHAPTER 36

GDP — CONSUMPTION

Have you ever heard people complain that we are a consumer society? Well, it's true. But if we weren't consumers our economic growth would be pretty miserable.

You see about 70 percent of all U.S. growth comes from the consumption of goods and services. This is why consumption is the most important part of U.S. GDP.

And if we ever stop being consumers, it could be a catastrophe for GDP!

Consumption is broken down into categories for different kinds of goods and services in the U.S. GDP report.

This overarching category of growth is technically written in the report as "personal consumption expenditures." And the two main categories for this, logically enough, are goods and services.

For goods, there are two main types that are important: durable goods and non-durable goods.

Durable goods are items that should ideally last for three years or more and are not consumed when you use them. Think about a car, washing machine, or a refrigerator. Those are all durable goods.

Non-durable goods don't last very long, and they're usually consumed with use like food, gasoline, and clothes. Of course, I do have some clothes that are more than three years old, but my wife won't let me wear them out in public.

Goods make up just a little more than one-third of total personal consumption expenditures, but services make up two-thirds of it! Services includes health care, recreation, food services, financial services, and a number of other services.

This is the work done by doctors, lawyers, massage therapists, economists, and manicurists.

Whether you're getting a pedicure or you've hired my firm to analyze your business. Those are both services. I'm just happy I don't work with feet.

Because consumption is the majority of the U.S. economy, the biggest risk to the U.S. economy is if there is a major shock to consumers — like in the Great Recession from 2007 to 2009.

Because consumer spending is so important, when it pulls back hard, you can get big drops in real GDP growth.

How does consumption look in the economy?

If consumption is good — if people have jobs and confidence is high — U.S. GDP is likely to be positive. And consumption is usually positive, as you can see in Figure 36-1.

This is one of the benefits of a service economy. It is also why a weakening labor market or weaker consumer confidence could weigh on this majority component of GDP. And it could be bad news for economic growth.

Figure 36-1: U.S. Consumption[1]

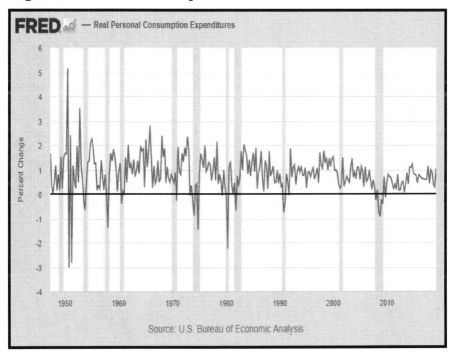

CHAPTER 37

GDP — INVESTMENT

You probably make investments: in your retirement account, in the equity of a home, or in your education. And you only make investments when you think they will pay off.

Businesses also make investments every time they buy a piece of equipment — like a forklift — or build a new warehouse.

Now, your personal investments in financial markets aren't a part of GDP, but business investments are! And that includes commercial offices, equipment, and intellectual property products like software and R&D.

While business investment is only between 15 and 20 percent of GDP, it is a big swing factor for overall economic growth, since it can drop like a stone or surge with changes in business confidence. And it's one of the four critical parts of GDP, officially called "gross private domestic investment."[1] This GDP category is comprised of three parts: investments businesses make, residential investments, and inventories.

One other caveat is that when we exclude inventories and talk about the investments businesses make and residential investments on their own, we call that "fixed investment." Houses, equipment, and warehouses are fixed — often literally to the ground.

But inventories can change frequently, like stores that stock up before Black Friday and holiday shopping but then stock out before New Year's.

Plus, business investment can generally swing hard and fast.

So, what drives business investment, and why can it swing more than consumption?

The truth is that business investment can swing, because far fewer people make decisions.

In the U.S. economy, with well over 300 million people, most people are consuming all of the time. But with business investment, there are often strategic decisions that can cause big pullbacks of investment immediately.

If the CEO of a construction company sees interest rates rising, that executive can pull back millions in investment with the click of a mouse.

This is compared to the 300 million people who will keep consuming unless their jobs disappear.

Look at it this way: If you are responsible for making investments in your business — like buying new computers or furnishing a new office — but the unemployment rate is rising or profit margins are falling, you don't want to be the one to go out on a limb. After all, you could end up cutting your own branch off with a saw and you'll get fired. Even CEOs can be fired by their boards.

You don't want to make a big recommendation to spend and then see the company lose money on its investment decisions.

Because if jobs get cut, you might be one of the first to go.

If the CEOs of the 10 biggest public companies decide to reduce their investment, this could negatively impact the investment part of GDP massively. And the economy could slow — or fall into a recession, which is when GDP growth is negative.

Economies grow when businesses invest. But businesses need to feel secure that consumption will be there.

Business executives and consultants like to talk about low-hanging fruit. Like a tree with apples that hang at a level that you can just reach up and pick them with no effort.

When an economy is growing slowly — like after a recession — businesses want to get new business that isn't expensive to get. It's easy, like fruit that hangs low on a tree.

Not much effort is good at that part of the business cycle — and business investment still holds back.

But as the economy strengthens and consumers regain confidence and spend more, companies are willing to make bigger investments.

They buy a stepstool to get a little more fruit, the apples a couple branches up — and then a ladder, and the next thing you know, they have a gold-plated, diamond-encrusted cherry picker going for the very last fruit at the top of the tree. And the economy is rocking.

Of course, I'm not really talking about fruit. I'm talking about incremental investment decisions that businesses make. When times are tough, they hold back on investment. And when times are good, they will spend money to make money.

How does your business feel about making investments?

Are they looking for low-hanging fruit, or are they ready to get out the gold-plated, diamond-encrusted cherry picker?

CHAPTER 38

GDP — NET EXPORTS

Trade is an important activity for every country — and it impacts your country's growth.

Whether you are Russia exporting oil, you are Germany exporting Mercedes, or you are the United States importing French wine.

You have to account for trade when talking about economic growth, because gross domestic product is the growth from new goods and services that are only *produced* inside the borders of a country. But since countries import and export, it's important to figure out the net amount of what is exported.

Net Exports = Exports Minus Imports

Net exports can be positive, when exports are bigger than imports.

But it can also be negative, when imports are bigger than exports.

Positive net exports are when exports exceed imports, and the level of net exports contributes positively to GDP. Conversely, negative net exports are when exports are smaller than imports, and that amount detracts from GDP.

France will count in its GDP French wine it exports to the United States. That adds to its net exports.

But the United States, where the wine is sold, will subtract the value of the French wine sold in the United States from U.S. GDP. After all, the wine is only a part of GDP in the country where it is produced.

And swings in trade can be pretty large.

In fact, trade can add or subtract 1.5 percentage points or more to growth in any given quarter.

If the economy should grow at 3 percent but next exports is very negative, it could pull down GDP by -1.5 percentage points. And growth will only be 1.5 percent.

Currencies can have an impact on what happens with exports and imports, which is why the value of the dollar or the euro can be important for GDP growth.

If the dollar weakens, it becomes more expensive for Americans to buy goods made overseas because you have to pay more dollars to buy the imports.

For example, French wine that used to be $10 could be $12 dollars if the euro rises 20 percent. For French wine, an extra $2 might not be a big deal.

But for a $50,000 German Mercedes, a 20 percent increase in the value of the euro would make it $60,000. That's an extra $10,000!

Yikes!

Since the prices go up, people buy less of them. This is why a weak dollar makes imports fall. It's more expensive to buy that Mercedes and wine.

The flip side of that currency impact is that the weak dollar can make U.S. exports seem cheap abroad, so U.S. exports — like Caterpillar equipment — are likely to rise, because they are cheaper for people in other countries to buy.

Just to recap: dollar down, imports down, and exports up.

That makes net exports bigger, which adds to GDP.

Of course, it works the other way too.

If the dollar strengthens, I can buy French wine more cheaply, which makes imports go up. It can also make a Boeing airplane more expensive overseas, and exports fall.

In this case, the strong dollar would actually reduce the amount of stuff produced in the United States, decrease our exports, and increase our imports.

Just to recap: dollar up, imports up, and exports down.

People say a strong dollar is good, but for net exports, it is not.

And lower net exports weakens GDP.

And these kinds of currency and trade dynamics are the same, whether we are talking about the U.S. dollar, the euro, the British pound, or the Russian ruble.

One key dynamic that impacts trade aside from currencies can be commodities — especially the import and export of oil and petroleum products like gasoline and diesel.

Sometimes spikes in seasonal demand (like in the summer for gasoline or winter for heating oil) can impact imports. And even hurricanes can disrupt trade flows and impact growth rates.

Trade Balance and Trade Deficit
The trade balance is the difference between exports and imports.

When exports exceed imports, and trade adds positively to GDP, this is called a trade surplus. On the other hand, when imports exceed exports, and trade detracts negatively from GDP, this is called a trade deficit.

A critical thing to know about U.S. net exports is that they are usually negative, and the United States usually runs a trade deficit, as can be seen in Figure 38-1.

That deficit detracts from overall economy growth, but it is also a hallmark of many developed economies.

Finally, it is also important to know that physical goods aren't the only things that flow in and out of countries and contribute to net exports. Services also are exported and imported, although in the case of U.S. services, trade is a much smaller dollar amount than goods trade.

Figure 38-1: U.S. Trade Deficit[1]

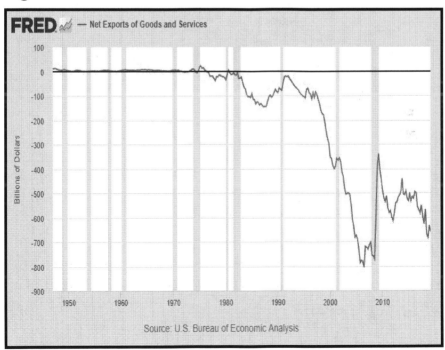

Services exports generally contribute positively to the U.S. trade balance, even though goods contribute more negatively to the trade balance. This means that even though the U.S. trade balance usually runs a trade deficit, U.S. services net exports prevent the U.S. trade deficit from widening even further.

Does your company engage in exports of goods or services?

Have you seen currency fluctuations impact trade in your business?

CHAPTER 39

GDP — GOVERNMENT SPENDING

Money the government spends comes from tax dollars — and sometimes from deficit spending, which is when the government spends money it doesn't have and borrows the money by issuing debt.

Whenever the government spends money, whether it is from taxes or debt, that money gets counted as part of economic growth — as part of gross domestic product, or GDP.

Government spending is one of the four main parts of economic growth as measured by GDP.

And these expenses are broken out into two categories.

First, there are federal (or national expenses and investments) for national defense and for nondefense. This would be aircraft carriers and federal government infrastructure spending like on highways.

Second, there are state and local expenses and investments. This usually includes schools, infrastructure, and other expenses.

In the United States, both categories of government contribute positively to GDP. And in total, these government expenses are between 15 and 20 percent of GDP.

Of course, the contribution of government expenses to GDP varies greatly by country. But it is usually a meaningful percentage.

Because politicians are focused on GDP, there's often an incentive to engage in deficit spending to boost the level of government expenditures to make GDP look bigger.

But there is a catch. Deficit spending today needs to be paid back tomorrow, so any boost of GDP from debt will be countered by a future lowering of GDP growth.

Put another way: When the government spends money it doesn't have and this gets counted as GDP, it's like you making a cash withdrawal off of your credit card — not your debit card but your credit card — and claiming that as income.

It's not income. It's something you have to pay back in the future.

The same thing is true with government deficit spending: It needs to be paid back. And the only way to do that is with more tax dollars, which weighs on growth.

There are also a number of important market impacts from increasing the U.S. national debt. In fact, financing more U.S. debt can weigh on the dollar, send the price of gold and precious metals higher (because these are prices in dollars), and also drive up interest rates.

Most economists agree that more debt weighs down the potential for an economy to grow in the long run, because of future tax obligations and the risk of rising interest rates on high levels of debt. And entitlements like Medicare, Medicaid, and Social Security present the biggest risks for increasing the national debt.

To summarize: Government spending is one of the four main parts of GDP. And there are incentives to spend more money than a government has, which is to engage in deficit spending. But this behavior results in rising debt payments and lower long-term growth potential.

In the United States, entitlements (Medicare, Medicaid, and Social Security) present significant economic threats to growth. This is a topic for a more substantive discussion in Chapter 55.

Monetary Policy

CHAPTER 40

MONETARY POLICY OVERVIEW

While children sometimes ask where babies come from, they're never going to ask you: Where do interest rates come from?

But it's an important question. Not for babies. But for you.

Interest rates come, in part, from central banks, like the U.S. Federal Reserve (a.k.a. the Fed).

And where does the data that drive their decisions come from?

Yep, you guessed it: economic indicators and reports.

In this section, we'll talk about the data behind central bank decisions that impact interest rates — something that affects you and financial markets.

Central banks implement policies that can impact every interest rate from your short-term savings account to 30-year mortgage rates.

You might have a mortgage, a car loan, or student loans. Higher interest rates make them all more expensive. Plus, some loans, like adjustable rate mortgages — adjust to changes in interest rates.

This matters because higher interest rates on a mortgage means that you'll be paying less for the house and more for the debt.

This also affects businesses that have lines of credit. When interest rates go up, businesses have to pay more in interest fees.

And if they need to pay more interest, they might decide to hire fewer people. Or they might need to lay some people off.

Because businesses and individuals pay more when there are higher interest rates, increases in interest rates can also send stock prices lower.

But lower interest rates give businesses and individuals more money to spend, which means that lower rates can send stock prices higher.

Let's say you own a moving company, and you need a loan to finance buying more moving trucks. You're going to buy fewer trucks if interest rates go up.

Now, I know what you're wondering: How do economic indicators fit into this whole interest rate thing? Why would your mortgage be going up? What could make your business loan be higher?

Since central bank decisions can either make or break your day, you need to know what data they are looking at to make their decisions. It could help you figure out ahead of time what they might do.

The good news is that central banks really only have two top priorities: inflation (which is how much prices rise) and unemployment (which is how many people do not have jobs but want them).

When business media people talk about these two goals for the Fed, they call it the *dual mandate*. You may have heard this on Bloomberg or CNBC, and now you know: It's the balancing of those two priorities — inflation and unemployment.

For the Fed, these priorities are roughly equal in their importance: 50/50. For other central banks, the priorities are different. For the European Central Bank, inflation is more important than unemployment.

But whatever the mix of priorities, central banks are all watching the economic indicators for inflation and jobs.

Their goal is to have a low but stable level of inflation that makes business investments and investor returns predictable while keeping as many people employed as possible.

This is a tough balance to strike because inflation rises when the labor market is tight.

You don't want an economy with no inflation and a 10 percent unemployment rate. And you don't want an economy with 10 percent inflation and a 2 percent unemployment rate.

There's a balance, which in the U.S. is a target of 2 percent inflation and around 4 percent unemployment.

As you can see, interest rates and inflation are important. And central bank views on these subjects are critical.

Fortunately, the Fed and other central banks also produce their own forecasts for future inflation, unemployment, and interest rates.

Check out the link I've provided to the Fed's calendar in the Data Appendix, which includes forecasts for all of these in the "Projection Materials." These can also be viewed here: **https://www.federalreserve.gov/monetarypolicy/ fomccalendars.htm**

CHAPTER 41

U.S. FEDERAL RESERVE DECISIONS

If you're thinking about buying a car on Tuesday and interest rates go up on Wednesday, that's bad news if you need a car loan.

Your monthly payment on that loan will be higher than it would have been just the day before. And you'll effectively be paying more for that same car.

The same thing happens to companies. If they are planning to buy equipment and interest rates rise, their monthly payments will rise too — and they might even decide to postpone making important purchases that would otherwise grow their business and create more jobs.

And you know what could make those interest rates go up on a single day?

A decision by the central bank in an economy to raise interest rates. In the United States, this means that a decision by the U.S. Federal Reserve.

And the Fed makes a number of important decisions, including about its main policy interest rate, known as the federal funds rate, which often impacts growth and inflation, as well as equity markets, the dollar, and bond prices.

The U.S. Federal Reserve makes decisions eight times per year at Fed meetings. Through 2018, four of these meetings entailed a release of quarterly forecasts of growth, inflation, unemployment rates, and even forecasts of the Fed's own future policy rates.

All Fed decisions are important, because they can impact interest rates.

But those Fed meetings that also include a release of Fed member forecasts tend to be more important.

After all, these are the Fed members' own expectations of what they will likely do with the interest rate policy that they set.

This data is collected from the actual members of the Fed — the people who make decisions about U.S. interest rates, which is why they carry weight.

This is why the most important part of the forecasts that are released by the Fed is the so-called "Dotplot."

You may have heard the term dot plot as a statistical depiction of numbers on a graph. But in the world of finance, markets, and interest rates, there is only one dotplot that matters.

It's the dotplot released as part of the Fed forecasts. And it's a chart that shows what Fed members expect the future federal funds rate will be in the future.

People on CNBC and Bloomberg will try to figure out which person is which dot — especially for outliers that are a lot higher or lower than the other members.

Honestly, some economists practically lose their minds over the dotplot — what they mean, who is which dot, and the overall distribution of the forecasts.

These dotplots and the other forecasts released by the Fed — including forecasts of GDP, unemployment, and inflation are important because investments will respond to them. If the Fed sees more inflation and expects higher Fed rates, the dollar will often rise, and stock prices can fall.

Beyond the impact on financial markets, Fed member forecasts can also be important because of their implications about the job market — and the economy. Their expectations can have important implications for your future career opportunities. Do you know what the Fed currently expects for the unemployment rate and the economy?

Fed meetings without forecasts are still important, but there is a lot more impact on markets when forecasts are released. Traders, investors, and corporate strategists watch Fed statements that accompany Fed decisions closely. With or without a dotplot.

CHAPTER 42

FED FORECASTS
AND THE DOTPLOT

Quantitative data sets aren't the only data out there, as can be seen with *The Robot and Automation Almanac.* In fact, qualitative data can be even more important — especially if there are reliability issues with some of the quantitative data you are working with, like government data that is subject to major delays or revisions.

It's important to know that quantitative data should not just be taken prima facie as the entire story. It is important to perform a certain level of testing and sampling on data that you are using in your analysis.

This is essentially a form of audit or due diligence that you have to perform on your data. Sometimes this can be done by testing and sampling the data set you have.

But a big part of this includes showing up and checking the facts in person. If it's corporate data, you should find out more about the collection process — and see some of it yourself.

I became an economist in 2004 for Wachovia Bank, which was absorbed into Wells Fargo during the financial crisis. Within a year, I gave a talk at the Philadelphia Fed, which can be seen in the Figure 42-1.

At the time I became an economist, Fed press releases were short. An example thereof can be seen in Figure 42-2. The trappings of current Fed meetings did not yet exist. In 2004, there were no press conferences at quarterly Fed meetings, as became the practice under Fed Chairman Ben Bernanke.

And there were no press conferences at every single Fed meeting, as has been only recently announced by Fed Chairman Jay Powell.

Figure 42-1: Speaking at the Fed in an Era of Less Data[1]

In 2004, there was also no release of Fed member forecasts. These are the so-called dot plots, which show a visual distribution of the expectations for federal funds rate, inflation, and GDP expectations that are held by members of the U.S. Federal Reserve's Federal Open Market Committee. Today, those forecasts are released every quarter.

Figure 42-2: Fed Press Release in January 2004[2]

Federal Reserve Release

Press Release

Release Date: January 28, 2004

For immediate release

The Federal Open Market Committee decided today to keep its target for the federal funds rate at 1 percent.

The Committee continues to believe that an accommodative stance of monetary policy, coupled with robust underlying growth in productivity, is providing important ongoing support to economic activity. The evidence accumulated over the intermeeting period confirms that output is expanding briskly. Although new hiring remains subdued, other indicators suggest an improvement in the labor market. Increases in core consumer prices are muted and expected to remain low.

The Committee perceives that the upside and downside risks to the attainment of sustainable growth for the next few quarters are roughly equal. The probability of an unwelcome fall in inflation has diminished in recent months and now appears almost equal to that of a rise in inflation. With inflation quite low and resource use slack, the Committee believes that it can be patient in removing its policy accommodation.

Voting for the FOMC monetary policy action were: Alan Greenspan, Chairman; Timothy F. Geithner, Vice Chairman; Ben S. Bernanke; Susan S. Bies; Roger W. Ferguson, Jr.; Edward M. Gramlich; Thomas M. Hoenig; Donald L. Kohn; Cathy E. Minehan; Mark W. Olson; Sandra Pianalto; and William Poole.

2004 Monetary policy

Home | News and events
Accessibility
Last update: January 28, 2004

A Fed release calendar from 2004 was quite sparse, as you can see in Figure 42-3. Back then, even Fed meeting minutes were released with a six-week lag, such that the minutes of a meeting were not released until the next Fed decision had been published.

Today, that is not the case. Fed meeting minutes are now released three weeks after a Fed decision is made. That's half the time. And it means that minutes are released before the next Fed decision is made public.

You can see the more robust Fed calendar from 2018 in Figure 42-4. As I mentioned above, the new calendars will include press conferences at every single Fed meeting.

So why has the Fed increased its publications and access?

Figure 42-3: Sparse Fed Calendar — Q1 2004[3]

March 25, 2004
   Minutes of Board discount rate meetings, December 15, 2003, to January 26, 2004

March 18, 2004
   Minutes of Federal Open Market Committee, January 27-28, 2004

March 16, 2004
   FOMC statement

February 5, 2004
   Minutes of Board discount rate meetings, November 10 to December 8, 2003

January 29, 2004
   Minutes of Federal Open Market Committee, December 9, 2003

January 28, 2004
   FOMC statement

2004 Press Releases:

This has a lot to do with fallout from the financial crisis. The Fed has greatly increased its transparency so markets will have more time to respond to changes in policy, which would hopefully provide for less market volatility — and could hopefully prevent another financial crisis.

That may be a lofty goal, but increasing transparency and creating more data should hold significant value for financial market analysts. The question is, does it?

Figure 42-4: Packed Fed Calendar — Q4 2018[4]

2018 FOMC Meetings				
January	30-31	Statement: PDF	HTML Implementation Note	Longer-Run Goals and Policy Strategy	Minutes: PDF	HTML (Released February 21, 2018)
March	20-21*	Statement: PDF	HTML Implementation Note	Press Conference Projection Materials PDF	HTML	Minutes: PDF	HTML (Released April 11, 2018)
May	1-2	Statement: PDF	HTML Implementation Note		Minutes: PDF	HTML (Released May 23, 2018)
June	12-13*	Statement: PDF	HTML Implementation Note	Press Conference Projection Materials PDF	HTML	Minutes: PDF	HTML (Released July 05, 2018)
Jul/Aug	31-1	Statement: PDF	HTML Implementation Note		Minutes: PDF	HTML (Released August 22, 2018)
September	25-26*	Statement: PDF	HTML Implementation Note	Press Conference Projection Materials PDF	HTML	Minutes: PDF	HTML (Released October 17, 2018)

There's a reason why this is the storyline in a chapter about how not all data is useful.

The Fed has gone to tremendous lengths to share its forecasts, its perspectives, its expectations, and its data. Even the length of Fed statements has increased significantly in the past 15 years, as you can see in Figure 42-5.

Figure 42-5: Fed Press Release in January 2019[5]

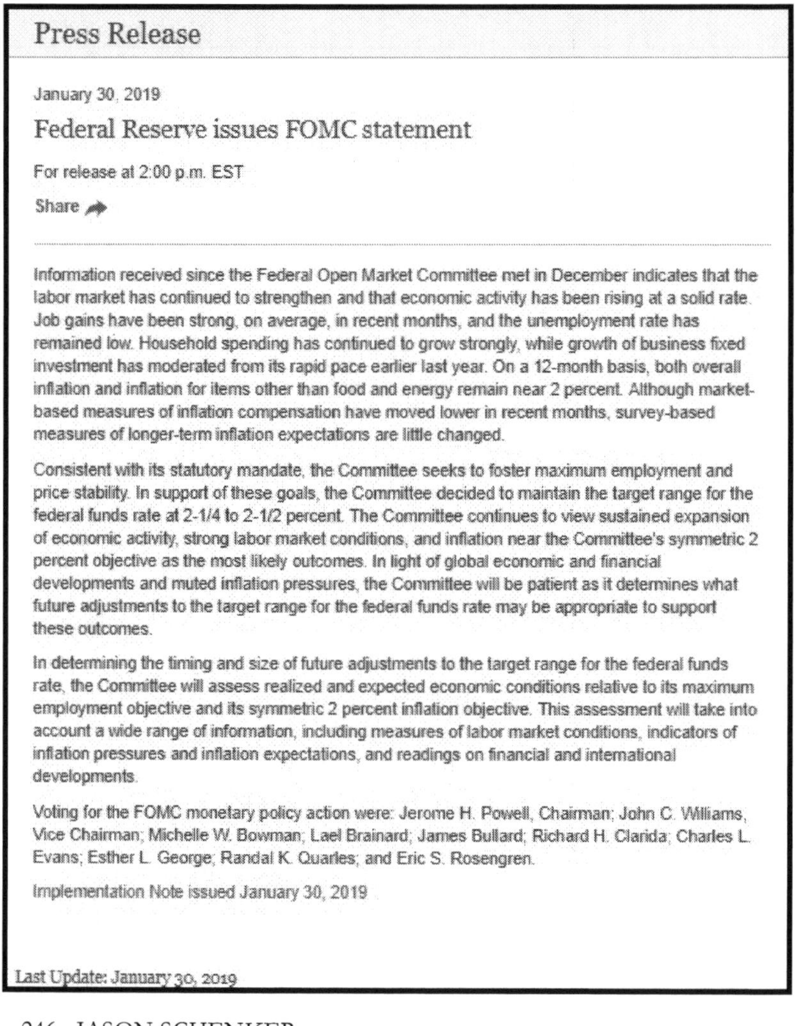

Press Release

January 30, 2019

Federal Reserve issues FOMC statement

For release at 2:00 p.m. EST

Share ➤

Information received since the Federal Open Market Committee met in December indicates that the labor market has continued to strengthen and that economic activity has been rising at a solid rate. Job gains have been strong, on average, in recent months, and the unemployment rate has remained low. Household spending has continued to grow strongly, while growth of business fixed investment has moderated from its rapid pace earlier last year. On a 12-month basis, both overall inflation and inflation for items other than food and energy remain near 2 percent. Although market-based measures of inflation compensation have moved lower in recent months, survey-based measures of longer-term inflation expectations are little changed.

Consistent with its statutory mandate, the Committee seeks to foster maximum employment and price stability. In support of these goals, the Committee decided to maintain the target range for the federal funds rate at 2-1/4 to 2-1/2 percent. The Committee continues to view sustained expansion of economic activity, strong labor market conditions, and inflation near the Committee's symmetric 2 percent objective as the most likely outcomes. In light of global economic and financial developments and muted inflation pressures, the Committee will be patient as it determines what future adjustments to the target range for the federal funds rate may be appropriate to support these outcomes.

In determining the timing and size of future adjustments to the target range for the federal funds rate, the Committee will assess realized and expected economic conditions relative to its maximum employment objective and its symmetric 2 percent inflation objective. This assessment will take into account a wide range of information, including measures of labor market conditions, indicators of inflation pressures and inflation expectations, and readings on financial and international developments.

Voting for the FOMC monetary policy action were: Jerome H. Powell, Chairman; John C. Williams, Vice Chairman; Michelle W. Bowman; Lael Brainard; James Bullard; Richard H. Clarida; Charles L. Evans; Esther L. George; Randal K. Quarles; and Eric S. Rosengren.

Implementation Note issued January 30, 2019

Last Update: January 30, 2019

But for all its efforts to create and share more information, the Fed may have done so in a way that creates more data than markets can digest. After all, there are currently four forecasts of GDP from the Fed available at any single point in time.

The four different forecasts of GDP available right now from the Fed are as follows:

1. Annual year-on-year GDP expectations from the FOMC, which is part of a quarterly release.
2. Atlanta Fed's GDPNow, which is a frequently updated model of expected quarter-on-quarter annualized growth in the next release of GDP.
3. New York Fed's NowCast, which is a frequently updated model of expected quarter-on-quarter annualized growth in the next two releases of GDP.
4. St. Louis Fed's Economic News Index Real GDP NowCast, which shows expected quarter-on-quarter annualized real growth in the next releases of GDP.

In a poignant statement about Fed policy, Janet Yellen noted at Jackson Hole, Wyoming, in August 2016 that "Our ability to predict how the federal funds rate will evolve over time is quite limited."[6] So, does all the data help? Maybe not.

For all of its data and transparency, the Fed only has so much control over imbalances, policies, and behaviors that could cause another recession. This doesn't mean that all the data is useless. But it cannot do the one thing that market mavens wish it could do the most: offer predictive insights into the future of the federal funds rate and other interest rates.

It's important to consider that the Fed struggles with making good forecasts, even though it has almost limitless resources and a massive staff of well-educated and highly skilled economists and econometricians.

The takeaway for working with data is that sometimes all the data in the world may not be enough to help you answer the questions you need answered. In other words, as advertised, not all data is useful.

CHAPTER 43

FEDSPEAK AND FED TESTIMONY

You don't need to run a trillion-dollar hedge fund to make the stock market move.

If you're the chair of the U.S. Federal Reserve System — the central bank of the United States — the weight of your words can cause the stock market to move significantly.

Just a hint of the potential to raise interest rates (and be hawkish) or leave interest rates low (and be dovish) can be absolutely critical for the expected cost of money, corporate profits, and growth expectations.

There are two main times when what the Fed chair says can impact markets: press conferences after Fed decisions about policy and testimony before Congress.

Let's talk about the Fed meeting press conferences. These take a standard structure: After a brief welcome, the Fed chair reads the Fed decision and then answers questions from the press in the audience.

Bloomberg, *The Wall Street Journal*, CNBC, and many others are there trying to put the Fed chair on the hotseat to reveal hints about future policy that are not in the written Fed statement.

And some investors and analysts try to dissect each and every word the Fed writes as well as every word said in these press conferences.

These people are usually called Fed watchers and the words from the Fed — said or written — are called Fedspeak.

This is why the impact of these press conferences can be significant, especially if the Fed chair says "too much." This has happened to more than one Fed chair. And it can move markets.

If the Fed chair hints at a timetable, even if it's an off-the-cuff guesstimate, financial markets take it as law. The reason: The Fed makes monetary policy — policies that can impact interest rates and growth in the economy.

The Fed has so much policy power, you'd be a fool not to believe!

Aside from press conferences, the Fed chair testifies before the House Financial Services Committee and the Senate Banking Committee, usually over a two-day period, twice per year.

Fed meeting press conferences are dominated by talking heads looking for a hot quote to put in the paper or talk about on TV.

But during testimony, the senators and congressmen who grill the Fed chair in Congress may be looking for the Fed chair to offer some sort of verbal snippet that they can use to justify an initiative they are pushing through the legislature.

Or they may be looking to find some testimony that justifies their opposition to certain policies from the presidential administration or others in Congress. Other times, the senators and congressmen may grandstand and discuss some economic plight, challenge, or concern of their constituents.

The goal of the legislators is similar to the press: Get the chair to say something edgy you can use later, like having the chair something about a change in healthcare while it's being debated in Congress.

The goal of the Fed chair is the same: Don't say too much.

And don't say anything with market implications that isn't completely measured because markets will move unintentionally.

And you might have to walk back your statement, causing another big swing in markets as they correct.

Especially big no-nos are any hints at a timetable for changes in the federal funds rate — the Fed's main policy interest rate — or any other changes of policy.

With one exception: if there is a perceived urgent need for a change in policy or a need to defend a change in policy.

This is something that happened when Fed Chairman Powell testified before Congress in mid-2019. With business fixed investment slowing, the Fed took on more dovish footing, and Powell was forced to defend the need for the Fed to potentially cut rates in the immediate term.

In general, Fed chair press conferences and testimony can be quite tense to watch, as the press and legislators are not on the Fed chair's side. They often have differing goals for their interactions, and they stand in opposition to the Fed chair.

CHAPTER 44

BALANCE SHEET POLICIES

One of the biggest challenges in the wake of the financial crisis was how to stimulate economic growth at a time of almost unprecedented slowing. Expanding central bank balance sheets was one of the unprecedented critical solutions that the U.S. Federal Reserve, the Bank of England, the European Central Bank, the Bank of Japan, and other central banks took to keep their economies afloat.

And as we think about the future of finance, it is important to know that the trend of ever-expanding central bank balance sheets has already started — and it is likely to continue in the future.

The fact that central banks have been able to conjure funds from the ether in order to buy various assets from mortgage-backed securities (MBS) and Treasuries to corporate debt and equities is disconcerting. But it was highly effective, and it is therefore likely to occur again in the future. After all, if it works, why stop now?

This reality supports some of the economic arguments in favor of cryptocurrencies.

In fact, the first Bitcoin transaction, which is often referred to as the Genesis Block, included the following message:

The Times 03/Jan/2009 Chancellor on brink of second bailout for banks[1]

The Bank of England engaged in multiple bailouts and a 300 percent expansion in the size of its balance sheet between 2007 and 2012, from around 94 billion British pounds to over 400 billion, as you can see in Figure 44-1.

Figure 44-1: Bank of England Balance Sheet[2]

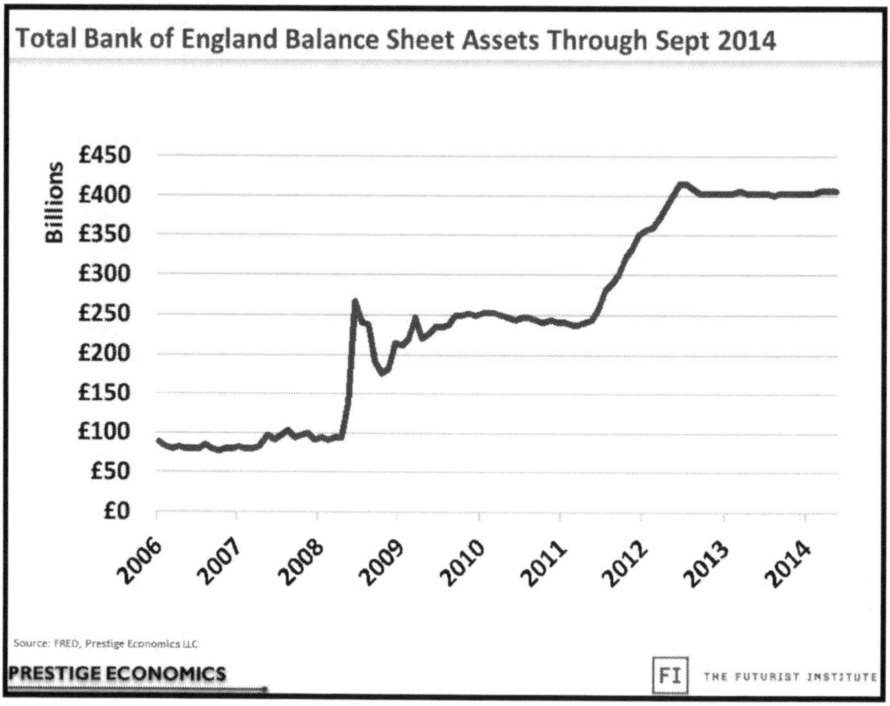
Total Bank of England Balance Sheet Assets Through Sept 2014
Billions
£450
£400
£350
£300
£250
£200
£150
£100
£50
£0
2006
2007
2008
2009
2010
2011
2012
2013
2014
Source: FRED, Prestige Economics LLC
PRESTIGE ECONOMICS
FI
THE FUTURIST INSTITUTE

But the Bank of England was not alone in taking these kinds of measures. The European Central Bank also increased its balance sheet massively. The ECB expanded its balance sheet from 1.3 trillion euros in January 2008 to 3.1 trillion euros in June 2012. Then, from June 2012 until September 2014, the ECB reduced its balance sheet by about one-third — letting it fall from 3.1 trillion euros to 2.0 trillion euros. This is in Figure 44-2.

During that time, however, the Eurozone economy slowed, and the Eurozone manufacturing PMI also conveyed a significant slowdown. The risk of a triple-dip recession in the Eurozone increased. As a result of this sharp slowdown, the ECB switched gears and rapidly expanded its balance sheet, which rose to almost 4.7 trillion euros by June 2019.

Figure 44-2: European Central Bank Balance Sheet[3]

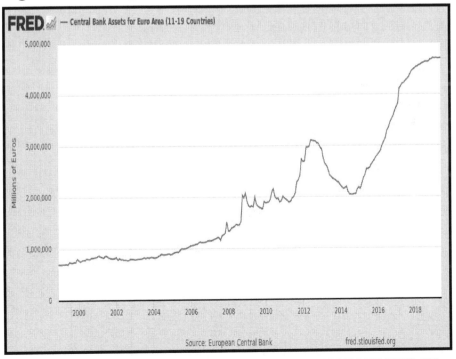

The expansion of central bank balance sheets was enacted as an extreme means to lower interest rates and indirectly stimulate financial activity and economic growth. This was achieved by having a central bank engage in buying government debt, mortgages, bonds, or equities. Each major central bank took a slightly different approach.

The most aggressive central bank expansion was implemented by the Bank of Japan (BoJ), and you can see the rise in total BoJ assets in Figure 44-3. In fact, the quantitative easing program has included significant purchases of Japanese real estate investment trusts, known as J-REITs, as well as exchange-traded funds, or ETFs, of Japanese equities as can be seen in Figure 44-4. In other words, the Bank of Japan has been a big buyer of equities.

Figure 44-3: Bank of Japan Balance Sheet[4]

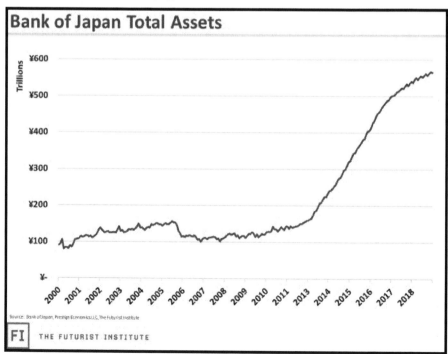

In 2010, the BoJ did not own any ETFs, but by March 2011, the BoJ's ownership of ETFs had increased to 185 billion Japanese yen. By September 2016, it had risen to over 11 trillion JPY. In September 2018, the BoJ owned almost 29 trillion JPY worth of ETFs. And the BoJ is now a major shareholder of many equities.

This situation is unprecedented and precarious, and it forces us to ask some difficult questions: How will the Bank of Japan extricate itself from Japanese equity markets? Will the BoJ ever be able to sell its equities? Will other central banks get themselves into a similar pickle? It is difficult to predict what will happen to Japanese equity markets if the BoJ steps back. But it does seem likely that other central banks could someday go down this path and buy equities as well.

Figure 44-4: BoJ Balance Sheet ETF Holdings[5]

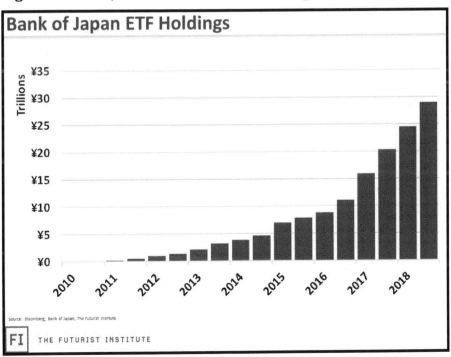

Bank of Japan ETF Holdings

Source: Bloomberg, Bank of Japan, The Futurist Institute

FI | THE FUTURIST INSTITUTE

The Federal Reserve

In response to slow growth after the Great Recession, the U.S. Federal Reserve engaged in purchasing mortgage-backed securities as a means to push down mortgage rates and stimulate housing activity in the United States. The Fed also purchased Treasuries, which pushed down interest rates — even after the federal funds rate was set by the Federal Reserve at zero percent.

As you can see in Figure 44-5, the Fed increased its balance sheet from around $900 billion in January 2008 to around a peak of $4.5 trillion by January 2015. But the Fed did not buy equities or corporate bonds, although it may consider doing so in the future. Presently, however, the Fed is focused on reducing the level of its balance sheet, which now still sits above $3.8 trillion. But the Fed is likely to expand its balance sheet in the future.

Figure 44-5: Total Fed Balance Sheet Assets[6]

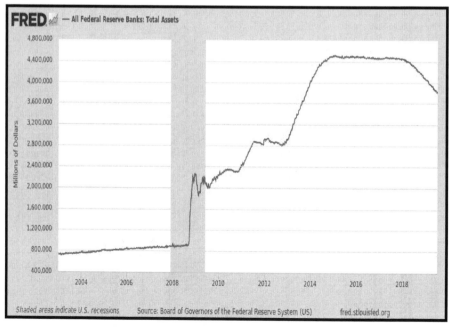

Beginning in October 2017, the U.S. Fed began reducing its balance sheet in a formal policy of balance sheet reductions by reducing reinvestment of maturing mortgage-backed securities and Treasuries. However, unlike the European Central Bank's attempt to reduce its balance sheet between 2012 and 2014, the Fed deliberately planned a very slow pace of balance sheet reductions. It was, I believe, in part due to the disastrous experience of the ECB that the Fed decided to be especially cautious in reducing the size of its own balance sheet.

The Future of Quantitative Easing

Even though the Fed has been reducing its balance sheet, the balance sheet is likely to remain at or near historically high levels for a long time to come. And it is likely to expand further in the future — rather than see declines down to levels seen before the Great Recession, which lasted from December 2007 to June 2009.

Expanding the Fed's balance sheet was highly effective at stimulating the U.S. economy. In other words, quantitative easing works. This means that the Fed is likely to expand its balance sheet again in the future.

Furthermore, Janet Yellen noted at the annual Kansas City Fed event in Jackson Hole, Wyoming, in 2016 that "I expect that forward guidance and asset purchases will remain important components of the Fed's policy toolkit."

She further added that "Future policymakers may wish to explore the possibility of purchasing a broader range of assets."[7]

In other words, the Fed is not just likely to engage in quantitative easing again in the future, but the Fed is likely to buy different kinds of securities in the future as well. Even though Fed policy got tighter in 2017 and 2018, it is likely to be much looser again in the future.

Central Bank Balance Sheets and Cryptocurrencies
The expansion of central bank balance sheets is fundamentally supportive of the economic and financial arguments in favor of Bitcoin and digital currencies that are not backed by central banks. The impact of the expansions and persistently high levels of central bank balance sheets of the ECB and the Bank of England is unclear.

What is clear, however, is that central banks have cracked open the QE cookie jar — and that they are likely to spend more money they don't have, effectively creating the ability to purchase assets out of thin air.

There is no problem, however, from an accounting standpoint, if the assets eventually expire in value and fall off the balance sheet. But that is not going to be the case with the balance sheet of the Bank of Japan, which includes significant equity assets.

As we look ahead to the future of finance and the future of quantitative easing, one of the things I often speak about is a risk that with each cyclical downturn in the future, central banks may continue to expand their balance sheets.

As long as they are all doing this, however, it may not drastically impact foreign exchange rates. After all, if everyone plays the game, it's tougher for there to be an outright winner — or loser.

And they will all want to play the quantitative easing game again if they can.

The Future Quantum State of the U.S. Economy

The dynamics I have just described could eventually result in something I refer to as the future quantum state of the economy. As the U.S. Federal Reserve buys more assets during each downturn with money that it pulled out of nowhere, the central bank's balance sheet will grow and grow.

And if former Fed chair Yellen's comments are to be believed, the Fed will eventually need to diversify the kinds of assets it buys, which could include everything from corporate debt to equities, as other central banks have done. But with each cycle, the central bank will become increasingly important as the buyer of last resort so that the U.S. economy becomes too big to fail.

This could also become extremely challenging, as the U.S. national debt rises due to unfunded entitlements and interest.

One potential worst-case scenario is where the central bank — after decades of cycles — eventually owns almost everything in the economy. And it will have paid for the debt, MBS, Treasuries, equities, and maybe even physical assets on its balance sheet with money it created — with money it didn't have in the first place.

This is effectively how we could have a quantum state of the economy, where the central bank owns everything with nothing.

Then we would have a big problem.

How central banks restore confidence in the fact that they won't go down this path will be a critical priority in the decade ahead.

And if they fail, this doomsday scenario could very well come to pass.

CHAPTER 45

FED GDP FORECASTS

There's a saying about economists: If you ask two economists about an issue, you should expect to get three opinions.

And the same is true even for economists of the U.S. central bank system — the Federal Reserve (otherwise known as the Fed).

In fact, there are four different Fed forecasts of U.S. economic growth, which is measured by gross domestic product — or GDP growth.

There you have it: one central bank, with four growth forecasts.

And the differences can be really important for you. Yes, you!

So how does that work? Well, like all central banks, the Fed makes important decisions about monetary policy, which usually involves interest rates and other activities that impact the interest rates people pay for mortgages, businesses pay on equipment, and the rates you earn on a savings account.

The Fed's growth forecasts impact those policies — and your money. Fed forecasts also impact trading activities, like buying and selling bonds or stocks. This means that your retirement account could go up or down depending on the Fed forecasts.

So, where do these four forecasts of growth come from?

Every quarter, Fed leaders produce forecasts of annual GDP for the current and coming years. These forecasts are released with Fed decisions.

In Figure 45-1, you can see an example of the FOMC GDP, inflation, interest rate, and other forecasts from June 2019.

Figure 45-1: FOMC GDP and Other Forecasts, June 2019[1]

Percent

Variable	Median[1]				Central tendency[2]				Range[3]			
	2019	2020	2021	Longer run	2019	2020	2021	Longer run	2019	2020	2021	Longer run
Change in real GDP	2.1	2.0	1.8	1.9	2.0-2.2	1.8-2.2	1.8-2.0	1.8-2.0	2.0-2.4	1.5-2.3	1.5-2.1	1.7-2.1
March projection	2.1	1.9	1.8	1.9	1.9-2.2	1.8-2.0	1.7-2.0	1.8-2.0	1.6-2.4	1.7-2.2	1.5-2.2	1.7-2.2
Unemployment rate	3.6	3.7	3.8	4.2	3.6-3.7	3.5-3.9	3.6-4.0	4.0-4.4	3.5-3.8	3.3-4.0	3.3-4.2	3.6-4.5
March projection	3.7	3.8	3.9	4.3	3.6-3.8	3.6-3.9	3.7-4.1	4.1-4.5	3.5-4.0	3.4-4.1	3.4-4.2	4.0-4.6
PCE inflation	1.5	1.9	2.0	2.0	1.5-1.6	1.9-2.0	2.0-2.1	2.0	1.4-1.7	1.8-2.1	1.9-2.2	2.0
March projection	1.8	2.0	2.0	2.0	1.8-1.9	2.0-2.1	2.0-2.1	2.0	1.6-2.1	1.9-2.2	2.0-2.2	2.0
Core PCE inflation[4]	1.8	1.9	2.0		1.7-1.8	1.9-2.0	2.0-2.1		1.4-1.8	1.8-2.1	1.8-2.2	
March projection	2.0	2.0	2.0		1.9-2.0	2.0-2.1	2.0-2.1		1.8-2.2	1.8-2.2	1.9-2.2	
Memo: Projected appropriate policy path												
Federal funds rate	2.4	2.1	2.4	2.5	1.9-2.4	1.9-2.4	1.9-2.6	2.5-3.0	1.9-2.6	1.9-3.1	1.9-3.1	2.4-3.3
March projection	2.4	2.6	2.6	2.8	2.4-2.6	2.4-2.9	2.4-2.9	2.5-3.0	2.4-2.9	2.4-3.4	2.4-3.6	2.5-3.5

Responses are collected and shown in a range, including a median and central tendency.

The Fed also forecasts other things, but the growth numbers are interesting, because three of the 12 regional districts in the Federal Reserve System — all produce forecasts of the current quarter's GDP level: Atlanta, New York, and St. Louis.

But how did we end up with multiple forecasts of GDP for the same quarter from the Fed?

Simple: The data is important and needed. There is no more important attribute to how an economy is growing than GDP, but it takes time to get all the data together.

Figure 45-2: FOMC Member Range of GDP Forecasts[2]

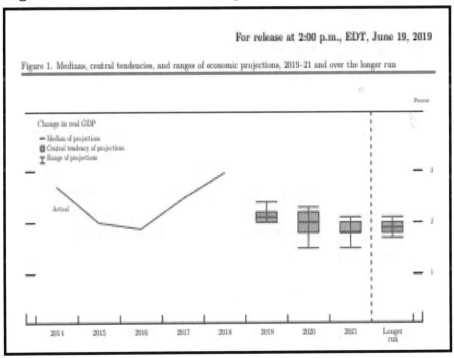

For the first quarter of GDP for a year — from 1 January to 31 March, the "advance" report of GDP won't be released until the end of April.

And then there will be two more releases: a preliminary GDP report at the end of May, and a third release at the end of June — at the very end of the second quarter.

This means that the final impacts of January aren't fully calculated and released in GDP until it's almost July and half the year is over.

This makes GDP data *old* in economic terms.

This has made forecasts of GDP by the Atlanta Fed, the New York Fed, and the St. Louis Fed important economic indicators to watch. These so-called Nowcasts for the current quarter's GDP are based on weather forecasts that try to predict the very near term.

Normally, people say that weathermen exist to make economists look good. But in this case, the approach of near-term weather forecasting has been applied to economic growth forecasts at the regional level.

This means that the regional Fed forecasts are based on short-term expectations, so they are updated after major economic releases.

Even though these banks have access to similar data and resources, there can be 1.5 percentage points or more differences between them.

Because of the wide range of estimates, you can call this data "noisy" — and not very useful. So, for now, traders are likely to pay the most attention to the official quarterly Fed forecasts that are released with Fed statements.

But short-term trading happens when these regional Fed reports are released — especially the Atlanta Fed Nowcast, which had established a slightly better track record through mid-2019 than the other measures.

Because Nowcasts use lots of data and are highly adaptive, their accuracy is likely to improve over time — and that would mean these reports could get more attention.

This also means that the stock market, the dollar, gold prices, and bond prices may become more sensitive to these Nowcast releases in the future.

CHAPTER 46

REGIONAL FED MANUFACTURING REPORTS

Talking about the national economy is all well and good, but you might really want to know how your region is doing.

Fortunately, these reports come from branches of the federal reserve system: New York and Philadelphia manufacturing indices have been the most closely watched historically, although other Fed banks also release indices, including Dallas, Richmond, and Kansas City.

It's very normal for companies that have operations in these regions to see their stock prices move on these reports — and sometimes the entire U.S. equity and bond markets can move on these reports as well.

First off, I need to clarify something: Manufacturing is a relatively small part of the U.S. economy — just a little more than 10 percent. But it is a capital-intense industry, and it has historically led economic growth in the United States.

This is why, even though the U.S. economy is clearly a service sector-focused economy, these reports matter.

Now, each of these reports has one big thing in common: They are data that is generated by survey responses from a number of participants across different industries in the Fed district in which the survey is conducted.

In Figure 46-1, you can see the 12 different Fed districts. And as I have noted, a number of these Fed districts release economic reports.

If these reports are weak, it can have two big implications.

Figure 46-1: Regional Fed Districts[1]

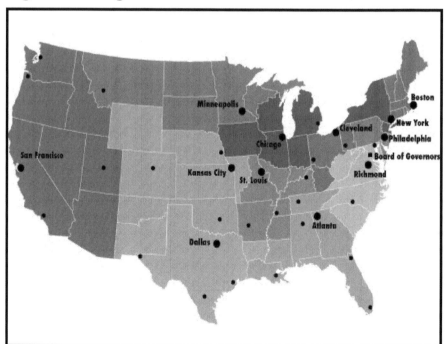

The first big implication of regional Fed manufacturing reports can be that economic activity is at risk in that region: In that region, companies could see profits fall (and maybe their stock prices too), jobs could be lost, home foreclosures could rise, and home prices could fall.

Not every Fed has a regional manufacturing survey, but if you live in a region with an index, you should be watching that data, because it could hit home in a big way.

In New York, you should be watching the Empire Manufacturing Survey. In Pennsylvania, you should be watching the so-called Philly Fed Index, which is compiled by the Philadelphia Fed.

In Texas, you should keep an eye on the Dallas Fed. In Kansas and the plains states, you should be watching the Kansas City Fed.

And in the Virginias or Carolinas, you should be watching the Richmond Fed Index.

I live in Texas and run a business in Austin. So, you can bet that I watch every monthly Dallas Fed report on Texas and the Dallas Fed district manufacturing, the service, and retail.

The second big implication of regional Fed manufacturing reports can be that economic activity is at risk nationally: This is especially true when all of the indices move together.

If one index falls, it could just be a regional blip — a hurricane, blizzard, or something else. But if all of these regional indicators fall, that's bad.

In that case, these regional Fed indices would serve as a proxy for the health of the overall economy. That can provide hints that the entire U.S. economy is at risk. That can also hurt stock markets and bond prices nationally.

Of course, the opposite is true as well. If these five indices are jamming, things are likely positive for the overall U.S. economy.

These reports also come out ahead of the ISM Manufacturing Index, which is the most important single leading economic indicator for the health of the US. economy.

So, naturally, investors and analysts want to watch economic data that could have important implications for the ISM. This is the second big reason to watch regional Fed manufacturing reports.

Regional Fed indices are important for regional business planning. And for your investments that might be tied to regional economic growth, construction, and manufacturing.

Inflation Reports

CHAPTER 47

INFLATION OVERVIEW

Do you remember when a can of soda was 25 cents?

Or maybe you just know someone who does?

What happened? Well, there's been inflation.

That's when there is a rise in prices across the entire economy over time.

Milk prices, home prices, car prices, and the prices of almost everything are higher now than they were 30 years ago.

The reason is inflation.

Inflation makes the prices rise for essentially all goods and services you buy. It means you can buy less stuff with the dollars you have. How much stuff you can buy with your dollars is called purchasing power. And when inflation happens, you can buy less stuff, and that's an erosion of your purchasing power.

It's why a dollar today, doesn't buy what a dollar used to buy!

This makes inflation a critical economic factor to watch for policymakers, traders, and for your own savings and investments.

Today, the ideal situation for businesses, banks, and the economy is when inflation is gradual, low, and stable.

You like to be able to predict if prices at the supermarket will be relatively consistent over time when you buy groceries.

And the same is true of most businesses when they think about making investments and buying equipment; they want to know roughly what prices will do.

This is why the goal of most central banks today is to see inflation around 2 percent per year.

Compared to historical levels, that's pretty low. In the early 1980s, inflation in the United States was over 10 percent per year. But even 10 percent per year is low compared to hyperinflation.

Hyperinflation is when inflation gets out of control and rises like crazy, with prices doubling, tripling, or rising by 10-fold. It can make money worthless quickly, and it is the biggest fear of every central bank.

There was hyperinflation in Germany in the 1920s, when over the span of less than a decade, the German mark weakened significantly. One dollar was worth only 4.2 marks, but just a few years later, one dollar was worth 4.2 trillion marks.

This wasn't because the dollar was so awesome. It's because hyperinflation destroyed the value of the mark. The value of each mark was worth one one-trillionth.

If you had saved money in your bank account, you would have been able to buy much less stuff with it, because the money in your bank account didn't become worth more — the prices of everything else just increased 1 trillion times.

A cup of coffee that would have been 1 mark could have been 1 trillion marks just 10 years later. Meanwhile, your bank account might have stayed unchanged at 10,000 marks. You could buy a lot of coffee at the beginning, and at the end, you wouldn't be able to buy a single coffee bean.

The currency became so worthless that people used mark bills for kindling and wallpaper.

There's even a story of a man who went to buy a loaf of bread with a wheelbarrow full of money. He went into the store to buy the bread and left his wheelbarrow full of money outside. When he came back out to get the money, the wheelbarrow was gone, but the money was still there.

Preventing hyperinflation is important. Because when prices get out of control, economic stability vanishes, fixed pension payments become worthless, and businesses become afraid to invest.

When this happens, economic growth slows sharply, and there's a risk of economic depression. You can even get political destabilization, which is what happened in Germany, where the Nazis came to power.

Fortunately, hyperinflation isn't very common, but it is most central banks' biggest fear. They watch for it in monthly reports of consumer inflation — what you and I pay for an average consumer basket of goods.

But central bankers also have another big fear when it comes to inflation: deflation. That's when the price of everything falls. That sounds really good, but it isn't.

Because deflation can make wages fall.

And that can also make fixed loan payments (like a mortgage or student loan) seem more expensive.

If your salary gets cut from $50,000 to $40,000 per year but your mortgage is still $1,500 per month, that will be a bigger percent of your income, and it will feel more expensive.

Deflation is also not very common, and it is usually a short-term phenomenon like when an economy weakens sharply — like in a recession or depression.

Inflation can impact your wages, your loan payments, the value of your savings, and the overall economy where you live. And if hyperinflation kicks in, it would be better to have wheelbarrows to drag your cash around in – than to have the cash itself. So, watch inflation closely!

CHAPTER 48

CONSUMER INFLATION

If you accidentally leave a dollar bill in your pocket when you do the laundry, it will come out wrinkled and it might be a bit faded, but it won't shrink.

Now, if you left that dollar bill in a pair of pants for a decade, you would find that it won't shrink — but its purchasing power will. You will be able to buy less stuff with that dollar, due to a general and persistent rise of inflation over time.

There are many different measures of inflation, and the most important measure is how inflation impacts consumers.

And one important measure of U.S. consumer inflation is the Consumer Price Index — or CPI — from the Bureau of Labor Statistics.

The CPI reflects price changes that are watched by executives, central bankers, traders, and the media — because its changes can affect interest rates, wages, and purchasing contracts.

Let's take a look at the consumer price index and what's in it —
especially the two headline figures the media and policymakers
watch closely: the total level of inflation (which is the blue line)
and what is called "core" inflation (which is the red line).

The total CPI includes everything in an average consumers'
representative "basket of goods." Food, energy, clothing, vehicles,
medical, shelter, and transportation.

While total CPI is one headline number to watch, central banks,
like the Fed, also watch something called core inflation, which
excludes food and energy. Both of these lines can be seen in
Figure 48-1, which shows year-on-year rates of inflation from the
monthly BLS report.

Figure 48-1: Consumer Price Index[1]

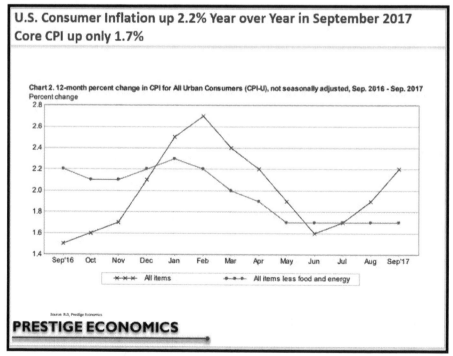

This isn't because Fed economists are robots that don't consume food or energy; it's because energy and food prices can see big swings — like the rise in gasoline prices after a hurricane, or grain prices after a drought.

And when looking at inflation, you want to remove those swings from your analysis.

Each CPI report is a huge document that comes out monthly, and it gets really down to the nitty gritty in terms of cost items, like:

- Differences in cost measures for pet food versus pet supplies
- Differences between the cost of wine at home and the cost of whiskey at home
- Differences between cookies and fresh biscuits, rolls, muffins.

In all of this data, there may be some categories that matter to you — or to your company — and those are worth watching.

I did a research project once for a cookie and biscuit industry group and had to compile and forecast some of this data to help them predict the future of cookie prices and how that might be different than biscuit prices.

Fortunately, there's even monthly data on this in the CPI report.

You can view a recent report here:
https://www.bls.gov/news.release/pdf/cpi.pdf

Companies care a lot about the CPI.

Some of my clients make cars and auto parts. And these companies use contracts for everything. They use labor contracts for workers — especially when there are unions.

And they also use purchasing agreements with vendors — where they agree to buy certain items at certain prices. Because inflation is a risk, many of these labor contracts and purchasing agreements are tied to CPI.

If inflation goes up, wages for workers go up in a way related to CPI, and the prices of goods purchased will also go up in a way related to CPI. By using official government numbers of the most widely cited measure of inflation — the CPI — companies and their workers as well as their vendors can come to terms on what the company will pay if inflation rises.

As someone who is paid to do a certain job, you need to make sure that your wages are rising every year by at least as much as inflation — otherwise, you are technically being paid less to do the same job.

A sharp rise of consumer inflation — especially core inflation — can push a country's central bank to raise interest rates.

Higher interest rates make a currency rise and equities fall, while lower interest rates make a currency fall and equities rise.

When inflation goes up and interest rates rise, it can cause a ripple effect across financial markets.

As for you and me, the impact of inflation is simple: When prices rise, the money you and I have is worth less than it was before.

CHAPTER 49

PERSONAL CONSUMPTION EXPENDITURES

Have you seen me shopping in a store recently?

If you have, chances are we weren't buying the same things. And this means that inflation will affect us differently over time, because we aren't buying the same "basket of goods."

Central bankers know this, which is why when they look at inflation, they try to capture a basket of goods that is being purchased not by you or me — but by everyone in the entire economy.

While the Consumer Price Index (or CPI) is one measure of inflation, the U.S. central bank – the Federal Reserve — prefers something called the personal consumption expenditures (PCE) measure of inflation.

That's because the PCE index covers a wide range of household spending — and the Fed views it to be more representative of inflation in the economy. The central bank thinks it's more "real," which means we need to talk about it.

This doesn't mean the CPI, which I discussed in the previous chapter, is no good. The Fed watches that too, and the CPI can be very important for labor and goods contracts.

But when it comes to central bank policy in the United States, the PCE is pretty much the only game in town.

The PCE is produced by the Bureau of Economic Analysis — the BEA — and its estimate of inflation is included in a report about personal income and spending (which are referred to as outlays) that is released every month.

The PCE shows the price increases that come from inflation in big categories of spending, like price increases in the costs of goods and services.

For goods, there are two main categories that are important: durable goods and non-durable goods.

Durable goods are items that should ideally last for three years or more and are not consumed when you use them. Think about a washing machine or a refrigerator. Those are durable goods.

Non-durable goods don't last very long at all, and they're usually consumed with use like food and clothes.

Services includes professional services — like accounting, legal, and financial services, as well as mani pedis, haircuts, and massages.

The PCE also has a core inflation figure that excludes food and energy to reduce the impact of volatile energy and agricultural prices.

That's the figure the U.S. central bank — the Federal Reserve — watches more closely than *any* other economic indicator, because it's viewed as the "real" level of inflation.

So, even if the CPI is more commonly discussed, even if it is more important for labor and manufacturing contracts, even if it's part of the U.S. tax code — it's the PCE that is the measure of inflation that matters most to the Fed. As such, more than any other inflation indicator, the PCE impacts what you will pay on car loans, if your employer will be purchasing new equipment, and how many euros you'll be able to buy with your dollars on your next trip to France.

Other economies have different measures of inflation, but there aren't too many countries that measure consumer inflation with multiple indices the way the United States does with the CPI and PCE.

The fact that these are just two of many different measures of inflation in the U.S. economy should underscore the importance of inflation.

Want to know what the Fed is going to next with interest rates?

The PCE is the key. And the Fed actually produces PCE and PCE Core forecasts in its projection materials every quarter.

If the PCE is likely to rise — so are interest rates, along with mortgage, car loan, and student loan rates.

Like the CPI, the PCE inflation numbers are released monthly. But perhaps more importantly, the PCE inflation numbers accompany an important growth report on personal income and personal spending. This data is important overall, because it reflects the monthly changes in consumption, which comprise about 70 percent of GDP. So the inflation data is mixed together with this critical growth data.

But most discussions about PCE — like this chapter — are really focused on the differences between CPI and PCE inflation.

For a full written and graphical depiction of the difference between the CPI and PCE, check out the link to analysis by the Federal Reserve of the Bank of Cleveland here: **https://www.clevelandfed.org/newsroom-and-events/ publications/economic-trends/2014-economic-trends/et-20140417-pce-and-cpi-inflation-whats-the-difference.aspx**

CHAPTER 50

PRODUCER INFLATION

I don't buy a lot of gasoline. I drive a small car, and I usually work remotely. So, you would think that oil prices might not be a big inflationary concern for me. But you would be wrong.

Big swings in oil prices matter to me, not just because I forecast them. They matter because they can drive the prices of other things up.

Unless you live on a deserted island or in an isolated pre-industrialized village that's been featured in a National Geographic documentary, chances are that almost everything you own was manufactured somewhere else. And that stuff had to be transported to you as well.

At every stage of manufacturing, physical goods are transported around. And that requires diesel for trucks or bunker fuel for ships. If oil prices rise enough, you might not just feel the pain of higher prices at the gas pump, you could feel it everywhere else too!

This kind of inflation most directly impacts manufacturers, and it's called producer inflation. It can impact every stage of a manufacturing process. And if stuff costs more to make, it will probably cost more to buy.

In the United States, producer inflation is measured by the Producer Price Index, otherwise known as the PPI report, which is released monthly by the Bureau of Labor Statistics.

While there is a big focus on consumer inflation by central banks, producer inflation is watched closely for a few different reasons:

First, major swings in finished producer inflation can have a leading impact on consumer inflation. In other words, a big rise of producer inflation this month could lead to a big rise in consumer inflation down the road. If the price of steel rises sharply, this could send up the price of a car frame, and that can send up the price of cars.

Second, producer inflation can erode company profit margins. While some of these impacts — like the higher cost of a car — will hit your wallet directly, it might not be as clear to the average person how producer inflation can pass through to send consumer prices higher — or how more producer inflation can hurt company profits.

In the PPI report, there are four stages of intermediate demand before getting to the final demand for a good or service — before getting to you.

We already talked about steel, so let's use car manufacturing with an aluminum part — like spinning rims — as an example to see how aluminum moves to the final demand through the four stages of the PPI:

In stage 1, there is goods production, like alumina and bauxite mining. These are minerals used to make aluminum — and they come out of the ground.

In stage 2, aluminum is fabricated.

In stage 3, auto parts are made from the aluminum. You need those spinning rims, am I right?

In stage 4, light trucks and cars are made from parts, including the aluminum parts in the third.

In the PPI, the price differences are recorded at each of these four intermediate manufacturing stages — as well as in the final demand stage, when goods, services, and construction are sold to final demand. In other words, it's the change in prices for that finished vehicle when it is sold to you.

One thing to know about the PPI is that even though there is a major focus on manufactured goods, there is also a measure of producer inflation for services.

Monthly changes in producer inflation are often influenced by big price swings in commodities — like swings in the price of steel, aluminum, or oil.

But the year-over-year producer inflation rates tend to be more important for telling a story over time. And that's what central bankers care about when determining policy: the smoothed-out story over time.

There are big differences between final producer inflation and consumer inflation.

Homeowners' equivalent rent isn't part of producer inflation, but it is part of consumer inflation.

And there are other differences.

If you want to dig in on the difference between the CPI and PPI, here is a report from the BLS: **https://www.bls.gov/ppi/ppicpippi.htm**

PPI reports are at the BLS website under: **https://www.bls.gov/news.release/pdf/ppi.pdf**

CHAPTER 51

ENERGY REPORTS

Energy prices are an important part of the U.S. inflation picture. And they are important for both companies that produce energy — and the companies that consume energy.

And there are U.S. energy reports about oil inventories, natural gas inventories, energy production, energy supply, and other dynamics in the U.S. and global energy markets.

Most important to know for U.S. inflation and the U.S. economy is that Americans have two times of year when energy demand is high.

In the summer, gasoline demand is high, because people go on summer vacations — and road trips. And in the winter, natural gas demand is high, because it's cold and natural gas is critical for heating demand.

But demand isn't the only thing that drives energy prices. Energy supplies are important for prices too.

This is why petroleum inventories of gasoline, diesel, crude oil — as well as inventories of natural gas — determine if prices will be high when demand is high.

And energy prices don't just impact what you pay for fuel at the gas pump or what you pay to heat your house or fireplace. Energy prices also impact the value of energy investments you may have. And energy prices impact inflation.

There are two important weekly inventory reports from the U.S. Department of Energy's Energy Information Agency that can influence energy prices:

The first report is the Weekly Petroleum Status Report, which is informally called DOE Oil Inventories. It is here: **https://www.eia.gov/petroleum/supply/weekly/**

The second report is the Weekly Natural Gas Storage Report, which is informally called the EIA storage report. It is here: **http://ir.eia.gov/ngs/ngs.html**

DOE Inventories
The DOE Oil Inventories include data about U.S. crude oil, gasoline, and distillates inventory levels. So you know, distillates include diesel fuel and heating oil.

When crude oil and other petroleum product inventories rise a lot, the appearance of more supply can weigh on oil prices. After all, supply up, prices down. And a drop in oil prices can weigh on oil company stock prices.

But if a weekly report shows a big drop in these inventories, that is often interpreted that supplies are tight. And when supply down, prices up.

Crude oil, gasoline, and diesel prices can rise on these reports, which is why the stock price of oil and gas companies, like Exxon or BP, may rise on a drop in supply in these weekly reports.

For an observer of energy markets, it is important to know that there is also a second weekly oil inventory report that some traders and investors pay attention to.

The first weekly oil inventory report that I have discussed so far is produced by the U.S. Department of Energy (DOE).

It is the "official" weekly oil inventory report.

The other weekly oil inventory report is produced by the American Petroleum Institute (API). Even though these two reports purport to show the same data, they often show massively divergent dynamics. Simply put, the numbers are often very different.

And the difference in reliability can be judged on the oversight of that data collection.

In my analysis of the two reports, I discovered that the DOE inventory report was subject to the rule of law — and that there could be criminal and civil penalties if the data provided are not accurate.

The instructions for the DOE form include the following caution:

> The timely submission of Form EIA-803 by those required to report is mandatory under Section 13(b) of the Federal Energy Administration Act of 1974 (FEAA) (Public Law 93-275), as amended. Failure to respond may result in a civil penalty of not more than $2,750 per day for each violation, or a fine of not more than $5,000 per day for each criminal violation. The government may bring a civil action to prohibit reporting violations which may result in a temporary restraining order or a preliminary or permanent injunction without bond. In such civil action, the court may also issue mandatory injunctions commanding any person to comply with these reporting requirements.[1]

Even the actual weekly crude oil stocks report form EIA-803 is headed with a stern warning that underscores the importance of providing data — true and complete data:

> This report is mandatory under 15 U.S.C §772(b). Failure to comply may result in criminal fines, civil penalties, and other sanctions as provided by law. For further information concerning sanctions and data protections, see the provision on sanctions and the provision concerning the confidentiality of information in the instructions. 18 U.S.C. §1001 makes it a criminal offense for any person to knowingly and willingly make to any Agency or Department of the United States any false, fictitious, or fraudulent statements as to any matter within its jurisdiction.[2]

The risk of committing a criminal offence, or being subject to civil or criminal fines and penalties, should be enough to ensure that the weekly DOE report forms are completely and accurately completed.

The API is an important industry group, but its oil inventory reporting forms do not have the backing and power of law. For this reason, I have encouraged my clients to ignore the API data when it comes to an examination of U.S. weekly oil inventories.

After all, there is no requirement to comply and provide weekly stocks data, nor are there any repercussions for providing false information in weekly API data collection.

This may be an extreme example of why it is important to ignore some data. But whenever you are looking at different data, it is important to consider if it is useful.

You don't have to squeeze every potential variable into financial models you are building for market or corporate data. But you do need the ones that make the model more accurate.

EIA Storage
Aside from the two weekly oil reports, we should also look at the weekly U.S. natural gas report from the Energy Information Agency.

The EIA natural gas report shows the total level of U.S. natural gas inventories. It also shows that level of inventories compared to the five-year average.

These figures are watched closely, and they can be seen in Figure 51-1.

The EIA weekly natural gas inventory report also shows levels of natural gas in parts of the United States.

Understandably, natural gas prices respond to weekly changes in inventories, especially when there are big increases or decreases.

Companies that largely produce natural gas — as opposed to oil — can see their stock prices rise and fall significantly with changes in this storage data.

Figure 51-1: Weekly Natural Gas Inventories[3]

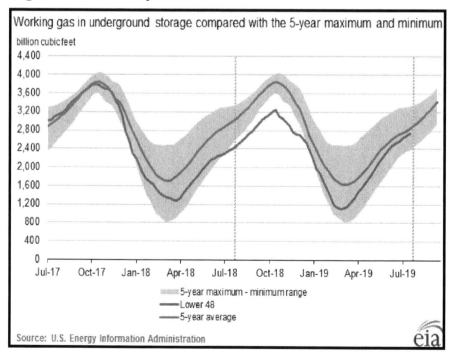

Natural gas inventories are most critical during the winter, because that is when the demand is highest — and consumption is driven primarily by the physical need to stay warm.

Sharp persistent inventory draws in the winter send natural gas prices higher. And this can be a real cause of concern in major cities that have limited pipeline capacity.

Very cold weather can make inventories fall sharply, making prices shoot up. But very mild winter weather can have less of an impact on inventories, making prices fall.

Natural gas price spikes can impact people's budgets, making them spend more on heat. Plus, natural gas can negatively impact company budgets.

Lower natural gas prices are better for the economy. They are more favorable for business budgets, and they are better for people's expenses in the winter.

Do you have investments in the energy space? They will be driven significantly by these weekly reports.

Or perhaps your company's profit margins shrink when oil prices or natural gas prices rise? If so, these would be important reports to watch.

CHAPTER 52

THE YIELD CURVE

Interest rates are what you pay on money you borrow: whether it's for a mortgage, student loan, car loan, or credit card.

But where do these interest rates come from?

Well, auto loans, mortgages, and bank savings account interest rates all come from something called the yield curve — which is the visual depiction of interest rates paid on government debt that goes out 30 years in the future.

Once you know what it is, you might want to look at the yield curve before getting your next mortgage or car loan. It's probably a good indication of whether you are getting a good deal, or if you are paying extra interest on those loans.

The yield curve is made up of U.S. government debt rates that go out 30 years. These are considered "risk-free" interest rates and these can be found at no cost on the Department of the Treasury website.

You can see this list of time periods from one month to 30 years.

These are the different rates for government debt for each of these periods. And these risk-free rates are important, because they are the foundation for other loans. That 30-year Treasury rate is tied to 30-year mortgages. The five-year and 10-year Treasury rates influence car loans, because auto loans are between five and seven years. And the one-month rate impacts how much money you earn from a savings account.

Below, in Figure 52-1, you can see where daily interest rates that comprise the yield curve can be found: **https://www.treasury.gov/resource-center/data-chart-center/interest-rates/Pages/TextView.aspx?data=yield**

Figure 52-1: Yield Curve Source[1]

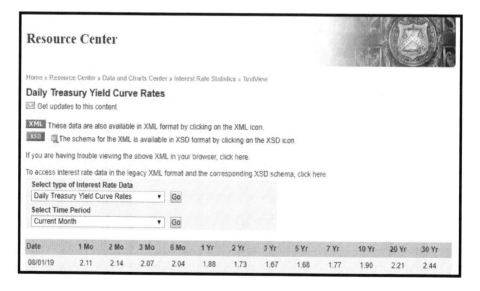

Finance professionals call this string of government interest rates in the future the yield curve. Some just call it "the curve."

Visually, these numbers can be put on a chart and connected to make a line or a curve of what government debt interest rates will *yield* over different time horizons out 30 years.

In Figure 52-2 is a graphical depiction of the interest rates on the U.S. government website from 1 August 2019. As you can see, some interest rates are close to the present, and others are much further out in the future. In the case of the yield curve at the time this book was published, part of the curve was inverted. This means that rates are not consistently rising across the curve.

Figure 52-2: Yield Curve Depiction[2]

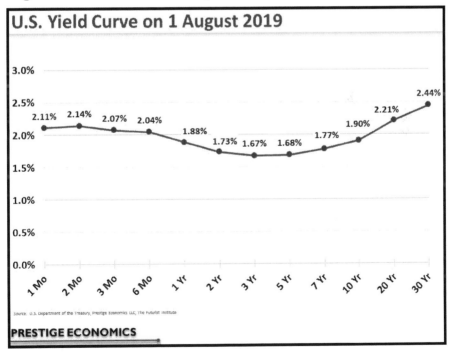

Source: U.S. Department of the Treasury, Prestige Economics LLC, The Futurist Institute

PRESTIGE ECONOMICS

Interest rates on one-month and three-month Treasury bills are called "the front of the curve." While interest rates for debt that matures much further in the future, like the 30-year Treasury bond, are called "the back of the curve."

A normal yield curve shows longer-term interest rates that are higher than near-term interest rates.

That makes sense, because if you loan me money for 30 years, I would expect that you'd want a higher rate of interest for such a long period, rather than if you loaned me money for only one year.

No matter how trustworthy I am, there is just more risk in the long run. And this is the logic used for interest rates of mortgages, bank loans, corporate bonds, and government Treasuries.

The longer the loan, typically the higher the interest rate.

For example, the interest rate of a 15-year mortgage is likely to be lower than a 30-year mortgage. Just by looking at the yield curve, you can see that the difference might be between one-half and 1 full percentage point. And on a mortgage that can be a lot of extra money.

1 percent on $300,000 is $3,000 a year. So for a 15-year mortgage, that would be $45,000.

But 2 percent on $300,000 is $6,000 per year. And in just the first 15 years of a 30-year mortgage, you'll pay $90K.

So that difference in interest rates can mean a *lot* of moolah.

Since it's normal that interest rates in the future are higher than in the present, if the yield curve is falling, that's a sign that the economy is expected to cool, and things are economically bad. People call this an inverted yield curve.

Check out the yield curve before getting your next loan. If your rates are wildly off from the curve, it could mean that you're just paying too much — or that you are viewed as a risky borrower.

If you know those answers, you can save a lot of money on your loans — especially a mortgage that you might have for 30 years.

Pulling Everything Together

CHAPTER 53

INFLATION SUMMARY

In 1995, I graduated high school and was offered a job for $45,000. Today, because of inflation, this would be $88,000.

Inflation impacts how far your dollars go — your wages, your savings. And it can impact interest rates that you pay on your mortgage too.

There are a lot of different inflation reports: consumer price inflation, personal consumption expenditures, producer inflation. These are just a few of the pieces in the U.S. inflation jigsaw puzzle.

So how do we reconcile this bonanza of inflation data?

Let's think of inflation in two parts: producers and consumers.

At the top is consumer inflation which shows up in the Consumer Price Index, which is known as the CPI.

Employers and manufacturers often use the CPI (consumer price index) in their contracts. This is also used in tax laws. As a "consumer" price index, it reflects what consumers pay.

Another measure of consumer inflation is in the personal consumption expenditures — or PCE — report. It's different from the CPI, but the U.S. central bank (the Fed) prefers the PCE, in making policy decisions.

In any economy, consumers are the top, and producer inflation feeds upward. Producers hit with higher prices either pass the prices up to consumers, or they absorb the costs and their profits shrink.

The Producer Price Index (or PPI) is a critical measure of U.S. producer inflation.

The inflationary pressures that attack the whole system —from all sides at both the consumer and producer levels are things like wage inflation and inflation from imports.

This can impact what a company pays its workers, and imports can impact producers and consumers.

There is a monthly reading of inflationary pressures on wages in the BLS Employment Report.

For imports, there is a monthly report for inflation on imports and exports in the Import and Export Price Index.

More import inflation can make it more expensive to buy auto parts from Canada and Mexico that go into a U.S. car for sale. And higher import inflation can also make you pay more for a bottle of French wine.

And there are other measures of inflationary pressures reported in business activity surveys — like the Institute for Supply Management's ISM Manufacturing and Non-Manufacturing Indices.

These inflation reports don't always go in the same direction. Sometimes, one measure of inflation can diverge from the others.

But exceptions aside, when the group of inflation indicators is rising (or falling), this has implications not just for central banks and interest rates but for wages and for the value of real assets — like houses and other property.

There are even some investments that are designed to benefit from higher inflation. And, of course, there are some that benefit from lower inflation.

How does your company monitor inflation?
Do you have investments that will gain value if inflation rises? What about if inflation falls?

Check out the links in the Data Appendix for a complete list of U.S. inflation reports — and where to find inflation data for other countries.

CHAPTER 54

WATCHING FOR RECESSION

The United States has been in an economic expansion since mid-2009. In July 2019, the current economic expansion will be the longest in the history of the United States.

But despite this strength, the question on many people's minds is, when will the next recession start?

After all, another recession is coming.

But that's just because another recession is always coming.

Recession Defined

Recessions have been traditionally defined by economists as two or more consecutive quarters of negative gross domestic product growth, otherwise known as GDP. During those two or more quarters, the level of GDP falls. This doesn't mean that GDP as a sum of consumption, government spending, investment, and net exports is negative; it means that the level of growth declines, which means the percent change from one quarter to the next quarter is negative.

The National Bureau of Economic Research (NBER) is a recognized authority on business cycle research in the United States, including the timing of U.S. recessions. Since 2010, the NBER has been using a slightly different definition of recession than the traditional definition involving two negative consecutive quarters of growth: "a recession is a significant decline in economic activity spread across the economy, lasting more than a few months, normally visible in Real GDP, real income, employment, industrial production, and wholesale-retail sales."[1]

The NBER defines itself as "a private, non-profit, non-partisan organization dedicated to conducting economic research and to disseminating research findings among academics, public policy makers, and business professionals," according to the NBER website at www.nber.org.[2]

The Federal Reserve Economic Database (FRED) of the St. Louis Fed uses the NBER definitions of historical recessions to determine the placement of shaded recession bars on FRED economic and financial graphs, as seen throughout this book.

Since the NBER definition of recession is good enough for the Fed, it's good enough for us! This is why I have used the NBER dates and definition of recession throughout this book.

A table of NBER recession dates can be seen in Figure 54-1.

Throughout this book, I have discussed leading economic indicators. And one of the most important things investors, executives, and individuals are watching for is recession.

Figure 54-1: Recession Dates According to the NBER[3]

BUSINESS CYCLE REFERENCE DATES	
Peak	Trough
Quarterly dates are in parentheses	
	December 1854 (IV)
June 1857(II)	December 1858 (IV)
October 1860(III)	June 1861 (III)
April 1865(I)	December 1867 (I)
June 1869(II)	December 1870 (IV)
October 1873(III)	March 1879 (I)
March 1882(I)	May 1885 (II)
March 1887(II)	April 1888 (I)
July 1890(III)	May 1891 (II)
January 1893(I)	June 1894 (II)
December 1895(IV)	June 1897 (II)
June 1899(III)	December 1900 (IV)
September 1902(IV)	August 1904 (III)
May 1907(II)	June 1908 (II)
January 1910(I)	January 1912 (IV)
January 1913(I)	December 1914 (IV)
August 1918(III)	March 1919 (I)
January 1920(I)	July 1921 (III)
May 1923(II)	July 1924 (III)
October 1926(III)	November 1927 (IV)
August 1929(III)	March 1933 (I)
May 1937(II)	June 1938 (II)
February 1945(I)	October 1945 (IV)
November 1948(IV)	October 1949 (IV)
July 1953(II)	May 1954 (II)
August 1957(III)	April 1958 (II)
April 1960(II)	February 1961 (I)
December 1969(IV)	November 1970 (IV)
November 1973(IV)	March 1975 (I)
January 1980(I)	July 1980 (III)
July 1981(III)	November 1982 (IV)
July 1990(III)	March 1991(I)
March 2001(I)	November 2001 (IV)
December 2007 (IV)	June 2009 (II)

CHAPTER 55

LONG-TERM
RISKS AND OPPORTUNITIES

One of the biggest challenges for the future of finance is the rising U.S. national debt. Every economist, FOMC member, and Fed chair warns about the negative impact high levels of debt are likely to have on long-term growth rates. But these warnings go largely unheeded, leaving dismal scientists to play Cassandra.[1]

The U.S. national debt is a growing problem. At almost $22.5 trillion, the national debt is not a small sum. In fact, it comes out to over $68,300 for every man, woman, and child living in the United States of America.[2]

That is a lot of debt!

As you can see in Figure 55-1, the pace at which the U.S. national debt is rising has accelerated. It took 205 years for the U.S. national debt to exceed $1 trillion, which happened in October 1981. But it then took less than five years for the national debt to double to $2 trillion in April 1986. The most recent doubling of the U.S. national debt occurred during the current business cycle — in the wake of the Great Recession.[3]

Although not as pronounced as the trend in total U.S. government debt, the debt-to-GDP ratio has also risen sharply since the onset of the Great Recession in December 2007 (Figure 55-2).

One major negative impact of a high national debt is the drag on potential future U.S. economic growth as measured by gross domestic product — or GDP. Plus, debt exposures can be exacerbated by compounding interest on already outstanding government debt.

Although some analysts are quick to note that the U.S. debt-to-GDP ratio is lower than other countries, it is also important to note that the U.S. economy is the largest in the world. This means that rising U.S. debt levels could make it more difficult for the global economy to absorb U.S. debt issuances over time.

2017 Tax Reform in Context

U.S. tax reform legislation that was passed in 2017 was lauded as a once-in-a-generation tax cut, which it was. While the reforms changed taxation laws, limits, and brackets for many different kinds of taxes, the legislation did not address entitlements. And payroll taxes were never discussed. Yet some of the biggest risks to the national debt and long-term potential GDP growth of the U.S. economy will hinge on addressing underfunded entitlements expenditures and fighting to contain the U.S. national debt.

To cover ballooning entitlements expenditures, payroll taxes could rise sharply, which could exacerbate the tax burden on workers, the self-employed, and people in the gig economy. This would not be a great look for the future of the U.S. economy.

Figure 55-1: Total U.S. Federal Debt[4]

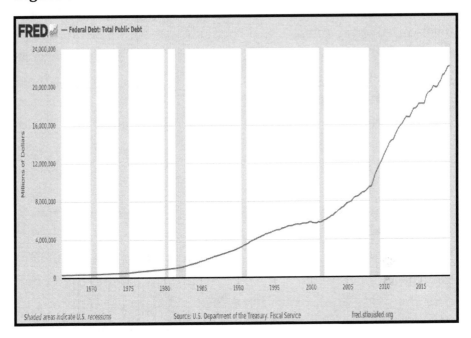

Figure 55-2: Total U.S. Federal Debt as a Percent of GDP[5]

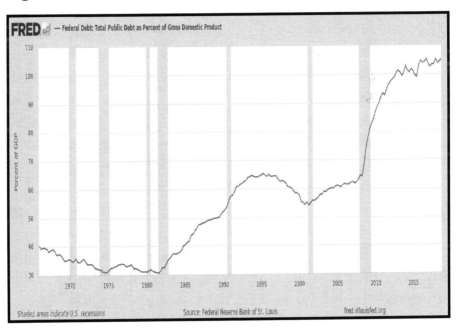

Without a reform of the entitlement system, increasingly high levels of government debt and changing demographics are likely to drive up interest rates and payroll taxes. Furthermore, a greater level of debt and higher payroll taxes could contribute to an acceleration of automation — and a reduction of jobs for people over time. Without a proactive approach, this could become unsustainable for the U.S. labor market, economy, and society.

These issues were not addressed by the self-proclaimed fiscally conservative Republican Party when it had control of both chambers of the legislature and the office of the presidency. This leaves me very concerned about prospects for these issues over the next decade. And it makes one thing seem certain: The 2020 presidential election is also unlikely to change these issues.

Risks of Debt

The problem with a rising U.S. national debt is that it can drive up interest rates. After all, as the supply of government bonds rises, the price will fall (as in all markets). And for bonds, when prices fall, interest rates rise. This means that over time, the net interest payments on U.S. debt are likely to rise. Allocating an increasing percentage of GDP to interest payments would clearly be bad for long-term potential U.S. GDP growth.

The risk of recession would further increase the likelihood that the debt level and the debt-to-GDP ratio would rise between 2020 and 2024. Even without a recession, the level of the national debt and the national debt as a percent of GDP are likely to rise significantly during the current presidential tenure.

And entitlements are a major source of additional imminent debt. Unfortunately, while the U.S. national debt is large, the unfunded financial obligations stemming from U.S. entitlements are much larger — and are likely to compound U.S. debt problems in coming years. Simply put, entitlements pose the greatest threat to future U.S. government debt levels — and U.S. economic growth.

Entitlements

U.S. entitlements, including Medicare, Medicaid, and Social Security, are financed by payroll taxes from workers. Payroll taxes are separate from income taxes, and while income tax rates have fallen on fiscal policy changes, payroll taxes are on a one-way trip higher. You see, entitlements are wildly underfunded.

All the sovereign debt in the world totals around $60 trillion.[6] That is the debt cumulatively held by all national governments in the world. But the size of unfunded U.S. entitlements might be more than three times that level. That's right: The unfunded, off-balance sheet obligations for Medicare, Medicaid, and Social Security could be $200 trillion.[7]

This level of off-balance sheet debt obligation existentially threatens the U.S. economy. The Heritage Foundation has taken calculations from the U.S. Congressional Budget Office about entitlements to create Figure 55-3, which looks quite catastrophic. Basically, by 2030, all U.S. tax revenue will be consumed by entitlements and the interest on the national debt. And these were the dismal calculations before tax reform and recent U.S. budgets started increasing the national debt even more rapidly.

The year 2030 is not that far in the future, and the clock is ticking.

But despite the magnitude of the entitlements problem, do not expect this to be an issue that will be seriously addressed during or following the 2020 presidential election.

The Grandfather of U.S. Social Security

Part of the problem with entitlements stems from their origins. The U.S. Social Security Administration website credits Otto von Bismarck as the grandfather of U.S. entitlements.[8]

Bismarck's portrait is even on the U.S. Social Security Administration's website (Figure 55-4).

Figure 55-3: Tax Revenue Spent on Entitlements[9]

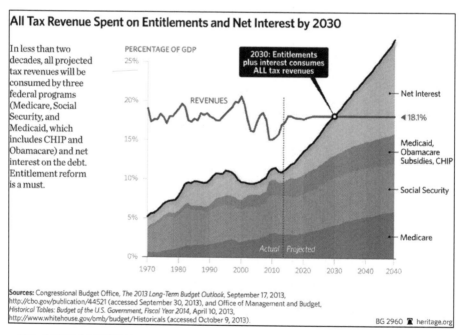

All Tax Revenue Spent on Entitlements and Net Interest by 2030

In less than two decades, all projected tax revenues will be consumed by three federal programs (Medicare, Social Security, and Medicaid, which includes CHIP and Obamacare) and net interest on the debt. Entitlement reform is a must.

PERCENTAGE OF GDP

REVENUES

2030: Entitlements plus interest consumes ALL tax revenues

Net Interest

◄ 18.1%

Medicaid, Obamacare Subsidies, CHIP

Social Security

Medicare

Actual Projected

Sources: Congressional Budget Office, *The 2013 Long-Term Budget Outlook,* September 17, 2013, http://cbo.gov/publication/44521 (accessed September 30, 2013), and Office of Management and Budget, *Historical Tables: Budget of the U.S. Government, Fiscal Year 2014,* April 10, 2013, http://www.whitehouse.gov/omb/budget/Historicals (accessed October 9, 2013).

BG 2960 ☎ heritage.org

Bismarck was a powerful politician known for his use of *Realpolitik*, a political doctrine built on pragmatism to advance national self-interests. For him, entitlements were convenient and expedient. Unfortunately, that is no longer the case. Today, entitlements threaten to crush the U.S. economy with increased levels of debt.

And without reform, they could decimate the U.S. workforce.

Bismarck's system was also sustainable. His system guaranteed a pension to German workers over 70, but the average life expectancy in Germany in the late 1880s was only 40.[10] In other words, so few people were expected to receive the benefits that the program's cost would be negligible.

Figure 55-4: Grandfather of Social Security, Otto von Bismarck[11]

Bismarck rigged entitlements to help crush his political opponents without having to pay out. But the current entitlement system in the United States is an unfunded off-balance sheet liability that threatens to crush the entire economy and usher in a labor market robocalypse. Plus, fixing entitlements presents a horrible dilemma as many Americans rely heavily on entitlements for income (Figure 55-5).

But how did this system break down? Bismarck had such a good thing going. What happened?

This can be answered in one word: demographics.

Figure 55-5: Expected Importance of Social Security[12]

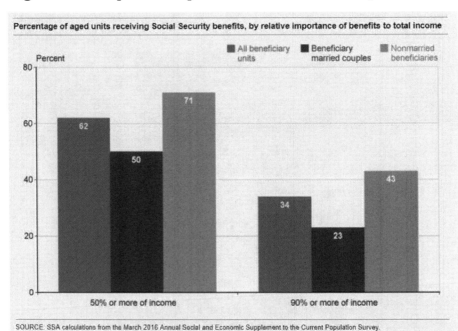

Percentage of aged units receiving Social Security benefits, by relative importance of benefits to total income

SOURCE: SSA calculations from the March 2016 Annual Social and Economic Supplement to the Current Population Survey.
NOTE: An aged unit is a married couple living together or a nonmarried person, which also includes persons who are separated or married but not living together.

Demographics

U.S. population growth has slowed sharply, and this demographic shift appears unstoppable. Plus, as birthrates have fallen, life expectancy has also risen. This compounds the funding shortfalls for entitlements. Worse still: No president, senator, or congressman can change U.S. demographics. This is bigger than one person.

And its discussion is unlikely to be anywhere near the 2020 presidential election — and other coming elections as well.

Population growth in the United States has fallen from annual rates of over 1.5 percent per year during the 1950s and early 1960s to just 0.7 percent since 2011.[13] Some of this slowing in population growth is due to a decline in the U.S. fertility rate. In general, fertility rates have been dropping globally, but according to demographer Jonathan Last, the U.S. fertility rate is still relatively high at 1.93.[14]

However, even though the U.S. total fertility rate is relatively high compared to other industrialized nations, it is below the 2.1 percent "golden number" required to maintain a population, according to Last.[15]

This is a huge problem for maintaining entitlements. After all, the entitlement system worked really well in 1940, when there were 159.4 workers per beneficiary (Figure 55-6). But it is more challenging since that number fell to only 2.8 in 2013. Plus, it is likely to fall to 2 workers per beneficiary by 2040.[16]

Entitlements are under siege from both sides: The birthrate has fallen — and life expectancy has risen.

In addition to lower birthrates, U.S. life expectancy has doubled since Bismarck implemented entitlements in Germany in 1889 — from around 40 years to above 80 years. Plus, the age at which people receive U.S. entitlements benefits has actually been lowered from 70 to 65. On top of a significantly larger population being eligible to receive entitlements, the medical costs required to support an aging population have also risen.

Figure 55-6: Ratio of Workers to Social Security Beneficiaries[17]

Year	Covered Workers (in thousands)	Beneficiaries (in thousands)	Ratio
1940	35,390	222	159.4
1945	46,390	1,106	41.9
1950	48,280	2,930	16.5
1955	65,200	7,563	8.6
1960	72,530	14,262	5.1
1965	80,680	20,157	4.0
1970	93,090	25,186	3.7
1975	100,200	31,123	3.2
1980	113,656	35,118	3.2
1985	120,565	36,650	3.3
1990	133,672	39,470	3.4
1995	141,446	43,107	3.3
2000	155,295	45,166	3.4
2005	159,081	48,133	3.3
2010	156,725	53,398	2.9
2013	163,221	57,471	2.8

Everything might be OK — if U.S. population growth were extremely robust. But it is not. Plus, the current administration is pushing hard to reduce illegal immigration to the United States. While this can have some benefits for society and the economy in some ways, it can also reduce the pace of population growth and lower the average U.S. birthrate.

Population growth has slowed to less than half the rate seen during the baby boom years, and the total U.S. fertility rate is below the "golden number" that is required to maintain a population. As Last notes, "Social Security is, in essence, a Ponzi scheme. Like all Ponzi schemes, it works just fine — so long as the intake of new participants continues to increase."[18] Unfortunately, entitlements are nearing a breaking point.

A big problem with slowing birthrates is the manifestation of a shrinking tax base at the same time that unfunded financial obligations are rising. This means that the unfunded $200 trillion or more in future entitlements payments will be borne by an increasingly smaller proportion of workers in the population. And as the population ages, there is another issue: Who will do the work? The answer is simple: We will create jobs for robots.

Payroll Taxes and a Shrinking U.S. Tax Base

When there is a tax shortfall, there is often a need to raise taxes. And there are risks of significantly higher payroll taxes in the not-too-distant future. Slowing population growth is likely to exacerbate U.S. debt and entitlement burdens by accelerating the reduction in the U.S. tax base — especially for payroll taxes, which fund entitlements. This could justify raising payroll taxes.

So, who pays payroll taxes?

Employees split entitlement costs with their employers, who pay half. This means that if entitlement costs rise, the cost for an employer to keep a person employed will also increase. The substitution effect of automation for labor would then likely accelerate because of the financial incentives in place for employers.

As payroll taxes increase to cover the costs associated with underfunded entitlements, the financial incentives for employers to shift work away from human laborers and add technology are likely to be reinforced. A number of my clients have shared their concerns about the risk of rising costs associated with health care costs for their workers.

How do you think employers will feel about the burden of paying much higher payroll taxes? They do pay half of them, after all.

Automation

As U.S. population growth slows and older workers age out of the workforce, automation could provide a solution. Automation has the potential to contribute significantly to U.S. economic growth.

But while automation solves some of the demographic problems we have in the United States, it threatens to exacerbate some of the entitlement problems. And unreformed entitlements present a significant risk of over-automation to the U.S. economy. If you were to think of the most important benefits you get as an employee, you might think of time off or sick days.

But your employer probably thinks about the most expensive items first: payroll taxes and health care. Kiosks and robots don't get time off, they certainly don't require health care costs, and they aren't subject to payroll taxes — for now.

In mid-2016, unemployment in Spain was around 20 percent,[19] and youth unemployment was around 43 percent.[20] So there were a lot of people available to work. But in Barcelona, Spain, during the summer of 2016, kiosks were in use at the airport's Burger King restaurant.

In Spain, as in much of Europe, the cost to hire someone can be prohibitive compared to the United States. And kiosks require no payroll taxes, no health insurance costs, no government entitlements, no vacation, and no sick days. With kiosks replacing workers, youth unemployment is unlikely to get significantly better. This also bodes ill for U.S. youth participation and unemployment rates. Be advised: Fast food robots (among others) are coming.

Entrepreneurs at Risk
Rising entitlement costs and payroll taxes could also stifle entrepreneurship. Unlike employees, who split payroll tax obligations with their employers, self-employed people bear the full brunt of payroll taxes personally. The rate is currently 15.3 percent of income.[21] In the future, that rate will rise faster for entrepreneurs since they will not be splitting the increase in payroll taxes with an employer. If entitlements are not drastically overhauled, a self-employment tax rate of 25 percent by 2030 is not inconceivable.

Increasingly high self-employment tax rates are likely to stifle entrepreneurship and hurt self-employed workers. According to an article by the Pew Foundation, the percent of workers who are self-employed fell from 11.4 percent in 1990 to 10 percent in 2014.[22] More importantly, the Pew Foundation notes that 30 percent of U.S. jobs are held "by the self-employed and the workers they hire."[23] In other words, in 2014, 14.6 million self-employed workers hired another 29.4 million workers, accounting for 30 percent of the entire U.S. workforce.

With the prospect of entitlement shortfalls and a shrinking tax base, self-employment tax rates are going to rise.

The impact of these additional costs is likely to engender a continued downward trend in the percent of self-employed workers. Plus, workers in the so-called gig economy — like all 1099s — are also subject to self-employment taxes. This could also make the existence of the gig economy less tenable in the future as payroll taxes rise.

The labor force participation rate is also at risk as the population ages further, unfunded entitlements rise, and the potential for overincentivized automation increases.

The labor force participation rate is a measure of what percentage of the able-bodied civilian population is working or looking for work. I also expect youth participation rates will continue to fall as younger workers are crowded out by older workers and automation.

Other Unfunded Obligations

As tax incentives present risks that workers could be crowded out by automation, consider also that the $200 trillion figure for unfunded entitlements does not take into account pension data for federal, state, county, or city government employees. Many of these workers also have defined benefits pensions that are underfunded — and in great need of reform. The gap in funds for these pensions will also likely incentivize automation and drive jobs for robots — rather than jobs for people.

There is an old joke that the best kind of autoworker to be is a retired autoworker. Without a reform of entitlements and defined benefits plans, the joke could be rewritten as the best kind of any U.S. worker to be will be a retired U.S. worker. This will affect all of us since unfunded off-balance sheet obligations could necessitate that government and private pension benefits be drastically reduced (especially for future generations) while contribution costs rise further. Problems beget problems.

Summary

Rising debt levels in the United States present long-term risks to growth. The surprise with the 2017 tax cuts was that despite Republican stewardship of the initiative, they were unbalanced.

As an economist, I see tax cuts as good. But I also see more debt as bad. Unfortunately, the tax reform of 2017 included both tax cuts — and more debt.

Plus, the most recent budgets during the current term of the Trump administration also included significant increases in the national debt. This means that even if Trump is reelected, there may still be a need to "pork up" future budgets.

In the longer term, declines in birthrates, increased longevity, rising health care costs, falling labor force participation rates, and overincentivized automation are likely to accelerate and exacerbate the problems of the U.S. national defined benefits programs known as entitlements — programs that worked best financially when the age at which one received benefits exceeded life expectancy by 30 years.

But the entitlements system was ignored during the 2016 presidential election, during the 2017 tax reform, and in the 2018 midterms. It is likely to remain ignored for as long as possible — and likely through the 2020 presidential election cycle.

The Future Impacts of Entitlements
Just because politicians want to play the game of see no evil, hear no evil, speak no evil does not mean that in fact there is no evil.

In truth, massive unfunded off-balance sheet debt obligations — à la entitlements — could eventually subvert stable Western financial systems, eradicating economic growth and introducing destabilizing factors that could subvert democracy itself.

Some reading this may see my views here as hyperbole. And believe me, I wish they were. But sadly, they are not.

In order to finance shortfalls no one wants to address, the eventual impact could be very painful — and it could come sooner than many expect — like in-the-next-decade-or-so sooner.

This means by 2030, payroll taxes may find themselves closer to 25 percent than 15 percent. And that could have a deleterious effect on American workers, U.S.-based corporations, and U.S. equity markets.

On a global scale, these problems are even worse in some European countries, which means that the problems we have been ignoring could drastically impact economic and business growth expectations globally — especially in consumer-driven service economies, where drastically reduced incomes of retirees could dovetail with significantly increased payroll taxes for prime-age workers.

For the future of the economy and financial markets, the impact of these risks cannot be understated.

CHAPTER 56

DATA CHALLENGES
AND CREATING DATA

There's a great line from the movie *The Untouchables* that makes me think about creating data. The film, which stars Sean Connery and Kevin Costner, includes a scene where the two are trying to cobble together a team of G-men to take down Al Capone.

At one point, Connery recommends that he and Costner seek out recruits from the policy academy. He offers up a kernel of wisdom to Costner, noting, "If you're afraid of getting a rotten apple, don't go to the barrel. Get it off the tree."

I think of this line all of the time when I'm working with data. Often, the exact and ideal data you are looking for may not exist. And that's when it's time to dream up what data you would like collected or created.

One data series and report that my company Prestige Economics created is the MHI Business Activity Index. It is a measure of monthly activity in the material handling industry, which is a core part of the U.S. and global supply chains.

The impetus behind creating a real-time monthly activity indicator was the fact that the government data for material handling was imperfect.

In many ways, the data does not closely mirror the industry, it is released with delay, and it is often released with massive revisions of 15 or 20 percent. Bear in mind that those are not revisions to forecasts, but revisions to numbers that have already been published as "official."

I have also worked with other industry groups to create data, conduct benchmarkings, and otherwise create data where none exists. Many companies do this as a brand-building exercise. And it is often highly effective!

If you find yourself looking through economic data and you don't see exactly what you need, chances are you might just need to look a little harder. There is, after all, a lot of economic data out there.

But in all seriousness, if you cannot find what you are looking for, you may need to strategize about how to create the data you want or need.

We live in a time where communication is easy and electronic surveys can be short but provide massive value. There is no reason why you should not begin creating the data you want to find the valuable insights you are searching for. For a more in-depth discussion of this topic, I would refer you to my book *The Fog of Data*.

It may not be an easy process, but it could be very worthwhile.

Good luck!

CONCLUSION

SEEING THROUGH
READING THE ECONOMIC TEA

I hope that *Reading the Economic Tea Leaves* has provided some important baseline understandings of the kinds of economic indicators out there — and which are the most important.

Of course, there are more indicators beyond those in this book. And new indicators are born all the time. Consider the MHI BAI by Prestige Economics, which at the time of this book's publication was a little more than four years old.

And newer indicators are likely to emerge as the economy, labor force, and financial markets change — as they continuously do.

As you seek to identify meaning from various economic indicators, it is important to keep in mind that some of the data are imperfect. They may be compiled from inconsistent or inappropriate cohorts. The data may be mismatched, and — as is the case for government data — the data may be subject to massive and frequent historical revisions. Plus, you will bring your own biases to any analysis, and you need to be careful of that.

This is particularly true when it comes to forecasting, where there is a major risk of moral hazard. This means that your personal biases, opinions, or interests may inadvertently impact your opinions. In essence, it is a conflict of interest that impacts the analyst. And it's something important to watch for, because the #1 job of any private sector analyst is to *not get fired*.

All of these concerns are topics I discuss in great depth in my book *The Fog of Data*. In that book, I share how to transition from understanding economics and data to becoming a forecaster.

And, of course, there are many other resources I would recommend for further learning. The most important resources are the actual numbers in the reports I've discussed in this book. And I have shared a comprehensive list of where to find various reports in the following pages.

Additionally, and beyond the numbers, the data and reports produced by the U.S. Federal Reserve have a lot of tremendously valuable content. And while I would normally tell a budding economist to look at the numbers and less at the words, if you are going to read any words at all, read the ones from the Fed!

Finally, I would recommend you take my LinkedIn Learning course on economic indicators. It is a weekly series that I created with LinkedIn to help people better understand the importance of economic indicators and how they impact your investments, your business, your career prospects, and your life.

DATA APPENDIX

U.S. Economic Indicators

1. Bureau of Economic Analysis
BEA produces reports on GDP and auto sales.
- Home page with all reports and data: www.bea.gov
- GDP reports and data: https://bea.gov/national/index.htm#gdp
- Supplemental estimates, including motor vehicle sales: https://bea.gov/national/index.htm#supp

2. Bureau of Labor Statistics
- BLS produces data on employment, inflation, and other topics.
- Home page with all reports and data: www.bls.gov
- All economic news releases: https://www.bls.gov/bls/newsrels.htm
- Inflation reports and data: https://www.bls.gov/bls/inflation.htm

3. U.S. Bureau of the Census
Census produces data on new construction, housing, and retail sales.
- New residential construction reports and data: https://www.census.gov/construction/nrc/index.html
- New home sales reports and data: https://www.census.gov/construction/nrs/index.html
- Retail sales reports and data: https://www.census.gov/retail/index.html

4. Conference Board
Conference Board produces data on consumer confidence, Leading Economic Indicators, and Help Wanted Online (HWOL).
• Consumer Confidence Report: https://www.conference-board.org/data/consumerconfidence.cfm
• Leading Economic Indicator Report: https://www.conference-board.org/data/bcicountry.cfm?cid=1
• HWOL: https://www.conference-board.org/data/helpwantedonline.cfm

5. National Association of Realtors
NAR produces reports on existing and pending home sales.
• All NAR reports and data: https://www.nar.realtor/research-and-statistics
• Existing home sales data: https://www.nar.realtor/research-and-statistics/housing-statistics/existing-home-sales
• Pending home sales data: https://www.nar.realtor/research-and-statistics/housing-statistics/pending-home-sales

6. Federal Reserve Economic Database (FRED)
Website with economic data and graphs for most economic data series: https://fred.stlouisfed.org/

7. U.S. Federal Reserve
U.S. Federal Reserve policy calendar, releases, and forecasts: https://www.federalreserve.gov/monetarypolicy/fomccalendars.htm

8. U.S. Energy Information Agency (EIA)
• Main EIA site with reports and data: https://www.eia.gov/
• Weekly oil report: https://www.eia.gov/petroleum/supply/weekly/
• Weekly natural gas report: http://ir.eia.gov/ngs/ngs.html
• Annual Energy Outlook (AEO) report: https://www.eia.gov/outlooks/aeo/?src=home-b1

9. Institute for Supply Management (ISM)
• Website for all ISM reports:
https://www.instituteforsupplymanagement.org/ISMReport/
index.cfm?SSO=1

International Data Sources

1. International Monetary Fund (IMF)
• All reports and data: http://www.imf.org/en/Data
• World Economic Outlook (WEO) database: http://
www.imf.org/external/ns/cs.aspx?id=28

2. Organization of the Petroleum Exporting Countries (OPEC)
• All reports and data: http://www.opec.org/opec_web/
en/21.htm
• Monthly reports: http://www.opec.org/opec_web/en/
publications/338.htm

3. Eurostat
• European economic data and reports: http://ec.europa.eu/
eurostat/data/database

4. Central Bank data and reports
• European Central Bank monetary policy:
https://www.ecb.europa.eu/mopo/html/index.en.html
• European Central Bank research and reports:
https://www.ecb.europa.eu/pub/html/index.en.html
• Bank of England monetary policy: https://
www.bankofengland.co.uk/monetary-policy
• Bank of England statistics: https://www.bankofengland.co.uk/
statistics
• Reserve Bank of Australia monetary policy: https://
www.rba.gov.au/monetary-policy/
• Bank of Canada main page: https://www.bankofcanada.ca/
• Bank of Canada publications: https://www.bankofcanada.ca/
publications/

ENDNOTES

Chapter 3

1. U.S. Bureau of Labor Statistics, Civilian Unemployment Rate [UNRATE], retrieved from FRED, Federal Reserve Bank of St. Louis; https://fred.stlouisfed.org/series/UNRATE, 17 August 2019.

Chapter 5

1. U.S. Bureau of Labor Statistics, "Employment Projections — 2016-2026." retrieved from https://www.bls.gov/news.release/pdf/ecopro.pdf on 23 August 2019.

Chapter 8

1. Data for Chinese Caixin Manufacturing PMI, Eurozone Manufacturing PMI, and U.S. ISM Manufacturing Index sourced from www.econoday.com.
2. Ibid.

Chapter 9

1. Data for U.S. ISM Manufacturing Index sourced from Institute for Supply Management.

Chapter 10

1. Data for U.S. ISM Non-Manufacturing Index sourced from Institute for Supply Management.

Chapter 11

1. Data for Chinese Caixin Manufacturing PMI, sourced from www.econoday.com.

Chapter 12

1. Data for Eurozone Manufacturing PMI sourced from www.econoday.com.

Chapter 16

1. "World Economic Outlook." Retrieved from www.imf.org.

Chapter 19

1. Board of Governors of the Federal Reserve System (US), All Federal Reserve Banks: Total Assets [WALCL], retrieved from FRED, Federal Reserve Bank of St. Louis; https://fred.stlouisfed.org/series/WALCL, 16 August 2019.

Chapter 20

1. "The Employment Situation — July 2019." Bureau of Labor Statistics Retrieved from https://www.bls.gov/news.release/pdf/empsit.pdf on 23 August 2019.
2. U.S. Bureau of Labor Statistics, Civilian Unemployment Rate [UNRATE], retrieved from FRED, Federal Reserve Bank of St. Louis; https://fred.stlouisfed.org/series/UNRATE, 22 August 2019.
3. U.S. Bureau of Labor Statistics, Civilian Labor Force Participation Rate [CIVPART], retrieved from FRED, Federal Reserve Bank of St. Louis; https://fred.stlouisfed.org/series/CIVPART, 27 August 2019.
4. U.S. Bureau of Labor Statistics, Average Hourly Earnings of All Employees: Total Private [CES0500000003], retrieved from FRED, Federal Reserve Bank of St. Louis; https://fred.stlouisfed.org/series/CES0500000003, 27 August 2019.

Chapter 23

1. U.S. Census Bureau, Advance Retail Sales: Retail and Food Services, Total [RSAFS], retrieved from FRED, Federal Reserve Bank of St. Louis; https://fred.stlouisfed.org/series/RSAFS, 23 August 2019.

2. Ibid.
3. U.S. Census Bureau, E-Commerce Retail Sales [ECOMSA], retrieved from FRED, Federal Reserve Bank of St. Louis; https://fred.stlouisfed.org/series/ECOMSA, 23 August 2019.
4. U.S. Census Bureau, E-Commerce Retail Sales as a Percent of Total Sales [ECOMPCTSA], retrieved from FRED, Federal Reserve Bank of St. Louis; https://fred.stlouisfed.org/series/ECOMPCTSA, 23 August 2019.
5. Statista. Retrieved on 11 May 2019 from https://www.statista.com/statistics/534123/e-commerce-share-of-retail-sales-worldwide/.

Chapter 24
1. U.S. Bureau of Economic Analysis, Light Weight Vehicle Sales: Autos and Light Trucks [ALTSALES], retrieved from FRED, Federal Reserve Bank of St. Louis; https://fred.stlouisfed.org/series/ALTSALES, 22 August 2019.
2. U.S. Bureau of Economic Analysis, Motor Vehicle Retail Sales: Heavy Weight Trucks [HTRUCKSSA], retrieved from FRED, Federal Reserve Bank of St. Louis; https://fred.stlouisfed.org/series/HTRUCKSSA, 23 August 2019.
3. U.S. Federal Highway Administration, Vehicle Miles Traveled [TRFVOLUSM227NFWA], retrieved from FRED, Federal Reserve Bank of St. Louis; https://fred.stlouisfed.org/series/TRFVOLUSM227NFWA, 11 May 2019.
4. Retrieved from https://bea.gov/national/index.htm#supp and http://tonto.eia.gov/dnav/pet/hist/LeafHandler.ashx?n=PET&s=EMM_EPM0_PTE_NUS_DPG&f=M.

Chapter 25
1. Board of Governors of the Federal Reserve System (U.S.), Industrial Production Index [INDPRO], retrieved from FRED, Federal Reserve Bank of St. Louis; https://fred.stlouisfed.org/series/INDPRO, 17 August 2019.
2. Ibid.
3. Board of Governors of the Federal Reserve System (U.S.), Capacity Utilization: Total Industry [TCU], retrieved from FRED, Federal Reserve Bank of St. Louis; https://fred.stlouisfed.org/series/TCU, 18 August 2019.

Chapter 27
1. U.S. Census Bureau and U.S. Department of Housing and Urban Development, Housing Starts: Total: New Privately Owned Housing Units Started [HOUST], retrieved from FRED, Federal Reserve Bank of St. Louis; https://fred.stlouisfed.org/series/HOUST, 18 August 2019.

Chapter 28
1. This map was retrieved on 23 August 2019 from https://www2.census.gov/geo/pdfs/maps-data/maps/reference/us_regdiv.pdf.
2. U.S. Census Bureau and U.S. Department of Housing and Urban Development, New Private Housing Units Authorized by Building Permits [PERMIT], retrieved from FRED, Federal Reserve Bank of St. Louis; https://fred.stlouisfed.org/series/PERMIT, 18 August 2019.

Chapter 29
1. U.S. Census Bureau and U.S. Department of Housing and Urban Development, New One Family Houses Sold: United States [HSN1F], retrieved from FRED, Federal Reserve Bank of St. Louis; https://fred.stlouisfed.org/series/HSN1F, 18 August 2019.
2. U.S. Census Bureau and U.S. Department of Housing and Urban Development, Median Sales Price of Houses Sold for the United States [MSPUS], retrieved from FRED, Federal Reserve Bank of St. Louis; https://fred.stlouisfed.org/series/MSPUS, 18 August 2019.

Chapter 35

1. This image consists of two different series.: GDP and GNP. These were sourced as follows:
U.S. Bureau of Economic Analysis, Gross National Product [GNPA], retrieved from FRED, Federal Reserve Bank of St. Louis; https://fred.stlouisfed.org/series/GNPA, 18 August 2019.
U.S. Bureau of Economic Analysis, Gross Domestic Product [GDPA], retrieved from FRED, Federal Reserve Bank of St. Louis; https://fred.stlouisfed.org/series/GDPA, 18 August 2019.

Chapter 36

1. U.S. Bureau of Economic Analysis, Real Personal Consumption Expenditures [PCECC96], retrieved from FRED, Federal Reserve Bank of St. Louis; https://fred.stlouisfed.org/series/PCECC96, 23 August 2019.

Chapter 37

1. U.S. Bureau of Economic Analysis, Gross private domestic investment: Domestic business [W987RC1Q027SBEA], retrieved from FRED, Federal Reserve Bank of St. Louis; https://fred.stlouisfed.org/series/W987RC1Q027SBEA, 23 August 2019.

Chapter 38

1. U.S. Bureau of Economic Analysis, Net Exports of Goods and Services [NETEXP], retrieved from FRED, Federal Reserve Bank of St. Louis; https://fred.stlouisfed.org/series/NETEXP, 23 August 2019.

Chapter 42

1. Personal photo collection of Jason Schenker. Taken Philadelphia., Pennsylvania.
2. U.S. Federal Reserve System. Retrieved on 21 February 2019 from https://www.federalreserve.gov/monetarypolicy/fomccalendars.htm.
3. Ibid.
4. Ibid.
5. Ibid.
6. U.S. Federal Reserve System. Retrieved on 21 February 2019 from https://www.federalreserve.gov/newsevents/speech/yellen20160826a.htm.

Chapter 44

1. "Genesis Block." Wikipedia. Bitcoin Wiki. Retrieved on 24 August 2018 from https://en.bitcoin.it/wiki/Main_Page.
2. Bank of England, Total Central Bank Assets for United Kingdom (DISCONTINUED) [UKASSETS], retrieved from FRED, Federal Reserve Bank of St. Louis; https://fred.stlouisfed.org/series/UKASSETS, 24 August 2018.
3. European Central Bank, Central Bank Assets for Euro Area (11-19 Countries) [ECBASSETS], retrieved from FRED, Federal Reserve Bank of St. Louis; https://fred.stlouisfed.org/series/ECBASSETS, 12 July 2019.
4. "Balance Sheets of the Bank of Japan and Financial Institutions." Bank of Japan, Retrieved on 24 August 2018 from https://www.boj.or.jp/en/statistics/category/financial.htm/.
5. Ujikane, K. and Toshiro H. (16 April 2019)."Veteran Investor With Family Pedigree Slams BOJ's ETF Buying." *Bloomberg.com*, Bloomberg. Retrieved on 12 July 2019 from www.bloomberg.com/news/articles/2019-04-15/veteran-fund-manager-with-family-pedigree-slams-boj-s-etf-buying.
This also involved data from "BOJ's ETF Purchases Expanding Steadily" Japan Center for Economic Research. Retrieved on 12 July 2019 from https://www.jcer.or.jp/eng/pdf/170706_report (eng).pdf.
6. Board of Governors of the Federal Reserve System (US), All Federal Reserve Banks: Total Assets [WALCL], retrieved from FRED, Federal Reserve Bank of St. Louis; https://fred.stlouisfed.org/series/WALCL, 12 July 2019.
7. Yellen, J. (26 August 2016). "The Federal Reserve's Monetary Policy Toolkit: Past, Present, and Future." U.S. Federal Reserve. Retrieved from https://www.federalreserve.gov/newsevents/speech/yellen20160826a.htm.

Chapter 45

1. U.S. Federal Reserve System. Retrieved on 22 August 2019 from https://www.federalreserve.gov/monetarypolicy/fomccalendars.htm.
2. Ibid.

Chapter 46

1. U.S. Federal Reserve System. Retrieved on 21 February 2019 from https://www.federalreserveeducation.org/about-the-fed/structure-and-functions/districts.

Chapter 48

1. U.S. Bureau of Labor Statistics Consumer Price Index — July 2019. Retrieved on 23 August 2019 from https://www.bls.gov/news.release/pdf/cpi.pdf.

Chapter 51

1. U.S. Department of Energy, Instructions Form EIA-803 Weekly Crude Oil Stocks Report. Retrieved 18 February 2019 from https://www.eia.gov/survey/form/eia_803/instructions.pdf.
2. U.S. Department of Energy, Form EIA-803 Weekly Crude Oil Stocks Report. Retrieved on 18 February 2019 from https://www.eia.gov/survey/form/eia_803/proposed/form.pdf.
3. U.S. Energy Information Agency. Weekly Natural Gas Storage Report. Retrieved on 23 August 2019.

Chapter 52

1. U.S. Treasury Department. Retrieved on 20 August 2019 from https://www.treasury.gov/resource-center/data-chart-center/interest-rates/Pages/TextView.aspx?data=yield.
2. Ibid.

Chapter 54

1. "US Business Cycle Expansions and Contractions." *The National Bureau of Economic Research*, NBER, 20 Sept. 2010, www.nber.org/cycles.html.
2. "About the NBER." *The National Bureau of Economic Research*, NBER, www.nber.org/info.html. 17 June 2019.
3. Analysis performed from: "US Business Cycle Expansions and Contractions." *The National Bureau of Economic Research*, NBER, 20 Sept. 2010, www.nber.org/cycles.html.

Chapter 55

1. Most recently Fed chair Powell noted this risk in July 2019 before Congress. Powell, J. "Semiannual Monetary Policy Report to the Congress." U.S. Federal Reserve. Retrieved on 12 July 2019 from https://www.federalreserve.gov/newsevents/testimony/powell20190710a.htm.
2. Retrieved from http://www.usdebtclock.org/.
3. U.S. Department of the Treasury. Fiscal Service, Federal Debt: Total Public Debt [GFDEBTN], retrieved from FRED, Federal Reserve Bank of St. Louis; https://fred.stlouisfed.org/series/GFDEBTN, 17 June 2019.
4. Ibid.
5. Federal Reserve Bank of St. Louis and U.S. Office of Management and Budget, Federal Debt: Total Public Debt as Percent of Gross Domestic Product [GFDEGDQ188S], retrieved from FRED, Federal Reserve Bank of St. Louis; https://fred.stlouisfed.org/series/GFDEGDQ188S, 17 June 2019.
6. Desjardins, J. (6 August 2015). "$60 Trillion of World Debt in One Visualization." Visual Capitalist. Retrieved 11 February 2017: http://www.visualcapitalist.com/60-trillion-of-world-debt-in-one-visualization/.
7. Mayer, J. (18 November 2015). "The Social Security Façade." Retrieved 11 February 2017: http://www.usnews.com/opinion/economic-intelligence/2015/11/18/social-security-and-medicare-have-morphed-into-unsustainable-entitlements.
8. U.S. Social Security Administration. "Social Security History: Otto von Bismarck." Sourced from https://www.ssa.gov/history/ottob.html.

9. Image provided courtesy of The Heritage Foundation. Retrieved 11 February 2017: http://thf_media.s3.amazonaws.com/infographics/2014/10/BG-eliminate-waste-control-spending-chart-3_HIGHRES.jpg.

10. Twarog, S. (January 1997). "Heights and Living Standards in Germany, 1850-1939: The Case of Wurttemberg" as reprinted in *Health and Welfare During Industrialization.* Steckel, R. and F. Roderick, eds. Chicago: University of Chicago Press, p. 315. Retrieved 11 February 2017: http://www.nber.org/chapters/c7434.pdf.

11. U.S. Social Security Administration. "Social Security History: Otto von Bismarck." Sourced from https://www.ssa.gov/history/ottob.html.

12. U.S. Social Security Administration. *Fast Facts and Figures About Social Security, 2017*, p. 8.*Retrieved on 17 June 2019: https://www.ssa.gov/policy/docs/chartbooks/fast_facts/.*

13. World Bank, Population Growth for the United States [SPPOPGROWUSA], retrieved from FRED, Federal Reserve Bank of St. Louis; https://fred.stlouisfed.org/series/SPPOPGROWUSA, 5 June 2018.

14. Last, J. (2013) *What to Expect, When No One's Expecting: America's Coming Demographic Disaster.* New York: Encounter Books, pp. 2-4.

15. Ibid., p. 3.

16. Last (2013), p. 109.

17. U.S. Social Security Administration. Retrieved 11 February 2017 from https://www.ssa.gov/history/ratios.html Last (2013) also uses a similar table in his book on p. 108.

18. Last (2013), p. 107.

19. Trading Economics. Spanish unemployment. Retrieved February 2017 http://www.tradingeconomics.com/spain/unemployment-rate.

20. Trading Economics. Spanish unemployment. Retrieved February 2017 http://www.tradingeconomics.com/spain/youth-unemployment-rate.

21. U.S. Internal Revenue Service. Retrieved from https://www.irs.gov/businesses/small-businesses-self-employed/self-employment-tax-social-security-and-medicare-taxes.

22. Pew Research Center. (22 October 2015). Retrieved 19 February 2017: http://www.pewsocialtrends.org/2015/10/22/three-in-ten-u-s-jobs-are-held-by-the-self-employed-and-the-workers-they-hire/.

23. Ibid.

ABOUT THE AUTHOR

Jason Schenker is the Chairman of The Futurist Institute, the President of Prestige Economics, and the world's top-ranked financial market futurist. Bloomberg News has ranked Mr. Schenker the #1 forecaster in the world in 25 categories since 2011, including for his forecasts of crude oil prices, natural gas prices, the euro, the pound, the Swiss franc, the Chinese RMB, gold prices, industrial metals prices, agricultural prices, U.S. non-farm payrolls, and U.S. new home sales.

Mr. Schenker has written 18 books and edited two almanacs. Five of his books have been #1 Bestsellers on Amazon, including *Commodity Prices 101*, *Recession-Proof*, *Electing Recession*, *Quantum: Computing Nouveau*, and *Jobs for Robots*. He also edited the #1 Bestseller *The Robot and Automation Almanac — 2018* as well as the 2019 edition of the almanac. Mr. Schenker is also a columnist for *Bloomberg Opinion*, and he has appeared as a guest host on Bloomberg Television as well as a guest on CNBC and other television media. He is frequently quoted in the press, including *The Wall Street Journal*, *The New York Times*, and *The Financial Times*.

Prior to founding Prestige Economics, Mr. Schenker worked for McKinsey & Company as a risk specialist, where he directed trading and risk initiatives on six continents. Before joining McKinsey, Mr. Schenker worked for Wachovia as an economist.

Mr. Schenker holds a Master's in Applied Economics from UNC Greensboro, a Master's in Negotiation from CSU Dominguez Hills, a Master's in German from UNC Chapel Hill, and a Bachelor's with distinction in History and German from The University of Virginia. He also holds a certificate in FinTech from MIT, an executive certificate in Supply Chain Management from MIT, a graduate certificate in Professional Development from UNC, a certificate in Negotiation from Harvard Law School, and a certificate in Cybersecurity from Carnegie Mellon University.

Mr. Schenker holds the professional designations ERP™ (Energy Risk Professional), CMT® (Chartered Market Technician), CVA® (Certified Valuation Analyst), CFP® (Certified Financial Planner), and FLTA™ (Certified Futurist and Long-Term Analyst). Mr. Schenker is also an instructor for LinkedIn Learning. His courses include Financial Risk Management, Recession-Proof Strategies, Audit and Due Diligence, and a weekly Economic Indicator Series.

Mr. Schenker is a member of the Texas Business Leadership Council, the only CEO-based public policy research organization in Texas, with a limited membership of 100 CEOs and Presidents. He is also a 2018 Board of Director member of the Texas Lyceum, a non-partisan, nonprofit that fosters business and policy dialogue on important U.S. and Texas issues. He is also the VP of Technology for the Texas Lyceum Executive Committee.

Mr. Schenker is an active executive in FinTech. He has been a member of the Central Texas Angel Network, and he advises multiple startups and nonprofits. He is also a member of the National Association of Corporate Directors as well as an NACD Board Governance Fellow.

In October 2016, Mr. Schenker founded The Futurist Institute to help consultants, strategists, and executives become futurists through an online and in-person training and certification program. Participants can earn the Certified Futurist and Long-Term Analyst™ — FLTA™ — designation.

Mr. Schenker was ranked one of the top 100 most influential financial advisors in the world by Investopedia in June 2018.

More information about Jason Schenker:
www.jasonschenker.com

More information about The Futurist Institute:
www.futuristinstitute.org

More information about Prestige Economics:
www.prestigeeconomics.com

TOP FORECASTER ACCURACY RANKINGS

Prestige Economics has been recognized as the most accurate independent commodity and financial market research firm in the world. As the only forecaster for Prestige Economics, Jason Schenker is very proud that Bloomberg News has ranked him a top forecaster in 43 different categories since 2011, including #1 in the world in 25 different forecast categories.

Mr. Schenker has been top ranked as a forecaster of economic indicators, energy prices, metals prices, agricultural prices, and foreign exchange rates.

ECONOMIC TOP RANKINGS
#1 Non-Farm Payroll Forecaster in the World
#1 New Home Sales Forecaster in the World
#2 U.S. Unemployment Rate Forecaster in the World
#3 Durable Goods Orders Forecaster in the World
#6 Consumer Confidence Forecaster in the World
#7 ISM Manufacturing Index Forecaster in the World
#7 U.S. Housing Start Forecaster in the World

ENERGY PRICE TOP RANKINGS

#1 WTI Crude Oil Price Forecaster in the World

#1 Brent Crude Oil Price Forecaster in the World

#1 Henry Hub Natural Gas Price Forecaster in the World

METALS PRICE TOP RANKINGS

#1 Gold Price Forecaster in the World

#1 Platinum Price Forecaster in the World

#1 Palladium Price Forecaster in the World

#1 Industrial Metals Price Forecaster in the World

#1 Copper Price Forecaster in the World

#1 Aluminum Price Forecaster in the World

#1 Nickel Price Forecaster in the World

#1 Tin Price Forecaster in the World

#1 Zinc Price Forecaster in the World

#2 Precious Metals Price Forecaster in the World

#2 Silver Price Forecaster in the World

#2 Lead Price Forecaster in the World

#2 Iron Ore Forecaster in the World

AGRICULTURAL PRICE TOP RANKINGS

#1 Coffee Price Forecaster in the World

#1 Cotton Price Forecaster in the World

#1 Sugar Price Forecaster in the World

#1 Soybean Price Forecaster in the World

FOREIGN EXCHANGE TOP RANKINGS

#1 Euro Forecaster in the World

#1 British Pound Forecaster in the World

#1 Swiss Franc Forecaster in the World

#1 Chinese RMB Forecaster in the World

#1 Russian Ruble Forecaster in the World

#1 Brazilian Real Forecaster in the World

#2 Turkish Lira Forecaster in the World

#3 Major Currency Forecaster in the World

#3 Canadian Dollar Forecaster in the World

#4 Japanese Yen Forecaster in the World

#5 Australian Dollar Forecaster in the World

#7 Mexican Peso Forecaster in the World

#1 EURCHF Forecaster in the World

#2 EURJPY Forecaster in the World

#2 EURGBP Forecaster in the World

#2 EURRUB Forecaster in the World

More information about Prestige Economics:

www.prestigeeconomics.com

DISCLAIMER

FROM THE AUTHOR

The following disclaimer applies to any content in this book:

This book is commentary intended for general information use only and is not investment advice. Jason Schenker does not make recommendations on any specific or general investments, investment types, asset classes, non-regulated markets, specific equities, bonds, or other investment vehicles. Jason Schenker does not guarantee the completeness or accuracy of analyses and statements in this book, nor does Jason Schenker assume any liability for any losses that may result from the reliance by any person or entity on this information. Opinions, forecasts, and information are subject to change without notice. This book does not represent a solicitation or offer of financial or advisory services or products; this book is only market commentary intended and written for general information use only. This book does not constitute investment advice. All links were correct and active at the time this book was published.

ABOUT THE PUBLISHER

Prestige Professional Publishing was founded in 2011 to produce insightful and timely professional reference books. We are registered with the Library of Congress.

Published Titles

Be the Shredder, Not the Shred

Commodity Prices 101

Electing Recession

Financial Risk Management Fundamentals

Futureproof Supply Chain

A Gentle Introduction to Audit and Due Diligence

Jobs for Robots

Midterm Economics

Quantum: Computing Nouveau

Reading the Economic Tea Leaves

Robot-Proof Yourself

Spikes: Growth Hacking Leadership

The Dumpster Fire Election

The Fog of Data

The Future of Energy

The Future of Finance is Now

The Promise of Blockchain

The Robot and Automation Almanac — 2018

The Robot and Automation Almanac — 2019

Future Titles

The Future of Agriculture

The Future of Healthcare

The Robot and Automation Almanac — 2020

Prestige Professional Publishing LLC

4412 City Park Road #4

Austin, Texas 78730

www.prestigeprofessionalpublishing.com

ISBN: 978-1-946197-42-9 *Paperback*

978-1-946197-49-8 *Ebook*

Made in the USA
Columbia, SC
06 September 2019